# MORAL LEADERSHIP
## IN A
# POSTMODERN AGE

# MORAL LEADERSHIP IN A POSTMODERN AGE

*Robin Gill*

T&T CLARK
EDINBURGH

T&T CLARK LTD
59 GEORGE STREET
EDINBURGH EH2 2LQ
SCOTLAND

First published 1997

ISBN 0 567 08550 3

British Library Cataloguing-in-Publication Data
A catalogue record for this book is available from the British Library

Typeset by Waverley Typesetters, Galashiels
Printed and bound in Great Britain by Hartnolls Ltd, Bodmin, Cornwall

✦

# Contents

v

150119

# *Preface*

This book struggles with a paradox: an age which views itself as increasingly pluralistic nonetheless appears to yearn for moral leadership. For a Christian ethicist this is one of the more curious features of postmodernity. I encounter it almost every day within the university world.

All of the chapters in this book have been written since coming to Canterbury in 1992. One of the great privileges of the Michael Ramsey Chair is that the holder is encouraged to travel throughout the Anglican Communion. I am most grateful to Archbishop Robert Runcie for establishing the post in this way and to Archbishop George Carey for his continuing support. It opens numerous theological doors and allows me to benefit from the wisdom of colleagues in many parts of the world. I am particularly grateful to Dr Bruce Kaye in Sydney, Dr Trevor James in Auckland, Professor Alastair Campbell then in Otago, and to Dr Per Hanson in Uppsala for invitations to give papers and to many other colleagues who have helped to shape and change my ideas. Earlier versions of some of the chapters have appeared in *Church Times* (chapters 6–8), *Theology* (chapter 5), *Studies in Christian Ethics* (chapter 3) and Jeff Astley and Leslie Francis (eds), *Christian Theology and Religious Education*, SPCK, London, 1996 (chapter 12).

Bringing together papers written for other occasions has inevitably caused a good deal of work trying to avoid repetitions, deviations and sheer contradictions – although some of the differing styles of the original papers have deliberately been retained. I had originally intended to write the long promised

*Moral Communities and Christian Ethics.* However, as I shall explain in the Conclusion, that would have been a mistake: it was important first to bring together two separate strands in my research, the empirical and the meta-ethical.

Finally my love once more to Jenny. My grasp of medical ethics would be very thin, and travel extremely empty, without her. Thankfully we now have identical lap-top computers which almost talk to each other and which can, if necessary, accompany us around the world. Whatever next?

# Introduction

Does morality ultimately depend upon faith? And, if it does, does this faith need to be religious faith? In the 1990s these have become important questions. A generation ago two contradictory claims were often made in the name of modernity. The first of these maintained that morality is simply a matter of 'feelings', 'emotions', or even just 'personal taste'. These feelings or emotions might be important for individuals, but they could have little to do with public policy. Morals in effect were simply a private matter. Alternatively it was just as often argued that morality can be established on purely rational grounds. These might be the grounds of utility or they might be the grounds of universally agreed principles. Essentially these grounds were regarded as being independent of faith of any kind – religious or otherwise.

Today many have become uncomfortable with such claims. The first was always the more vulnerable. Faced with some of the outrages of the twentieth century it has become increasingly difficult to maintain that morality is simply a matter of private emotions, feelings or taste. To depict moral outrage at the degradations of the Holocaust, at the many attempts at genocide in the twentieth century, at child abuse or at systematic torture, as simply a matter of 'bad feeling' or, even worse, as 'bad taste' seems wholly inadequate. For most of us these are the sort of evils that people simply *ought* to know to be morally wrong if they are responsible human beings. These are not just matters of personal emotion, feeling or taste – about which, apparently, there can be no argument – they are actually wrong in some objective sense.

But what is this objective sense? At this point the belief has often been expressed – essentially the modernist belief – that morality can be established on purely rational grounds. That is, morality can be established on grounds that are quite independent both of religious faith and of religious communities. It is frequently maintained that humanists have just as strong moral commitments as religious believers, but that humanists have the advantage of not basing these commitments upon any supernatural faith. They rely instead solely upon rational grounds which can be demonstrated objectively.

Unfortunately there are two quite distinct versions of such rational grounds on offer – one based upon principles and the other upon consequences – and the adequacy of both of them has been severely undermined by Alasdair MacIntyre's extraordinarily powerful book *After Virtue*. Writing from within the tradition of moral philosophy MacIntyre has challenged his fellow professionals to tell him what these purely rational grounds for morality might be. He notes that, after more than two centuries of debate about the relative merits of establishing morality either through principles or through consequences, there is still no agreement amongst moral philosophers. They can still find no way of resolving major differences on such issues as abortion or social justice. For example, one 'rational' group claims the right to life of the unborn child, whilst another claims the right of the woman to control her own body. One 'rational' group understands social justice in terms of inalienable principles, whilst another argues instead about public utility. These are differences that continue to divide us as a society (I will illustrate this later in relation to the current debate about euthanasia). MacIntyre can see no secular, rational way of resolving them. And in the absence of such a way he fears that might will become right – those with power will become the determiners of what is 'right'.

This argument has led MacIntyre in an increasingly postmodern direction, arguing that morality depends upon moral communities and upon traditions beyond individualistic reason. In turn this has led to his own return to the Roman

Catholic Church and to argue in his famous concluding paragraph of *After Virtue* that, 'what matters at this stage is the construction of local forms of community within which civility and the intellectual and moral life can be sustained through the new dark ages which are already upon us'.[1] It has also led him to co-operate with other concerned, Christian intellectuals, such as the celebrated American sociologist Robert Bellah. What is the moral basis of society? And how do moral communities within society contribute to this? These are the themes of Bellah's influential studies *Habits of the Heart*[2] and *The Good Society*.[3]

Of course, MacIntyre's position can be exaggerated. Churches do not always make very credible moral communities and there are manifestly moral communities which explicitly deny any religious belief. The British Humanist Society, for example, although very small has always had members who are deeply and passionately moral whilst denying any theistic beliefs. It is also evident that some of the most active moral lobby groups in this country at the moment – for example, animal rights activists – consist of a mixture of those who are and those who are not religiously committed. It would be a risky business for any group to claim a monopoly of moral commitment let alone moral purity.

One postmodern response to all of this is to argue that Christian ethics is a problem-solving discipline. The ethicist, by virtue of being a Christian, is enabled to solve ethical dilemmas which simply elude the secularist. Whatever the moral behaviour of Christians or secularists, Christian ethics as such is seen as the way to cut through troublesome moral knots. Whatever problems philosophers may have on particular moral issues, the Christian is fortunately delivered from these. So on a major ethical issue facing the world at the end of the millennium, Christians are enabled to resolve each issue using

[1] Alasdair MacIntyre, *After Virtue*, Duckworth, London, 1985 (2nd Ed.), p. 263.
[2] R. N. Bellah, R. Madsen, W. M. Sullivan, A. Swindler, S. M. Tipton, *Habits of the Heart*, University of California Press, Berkeley, 1985.
[3] R. N. Bellah, R. Madsen, W. M. Sullivan, A. Swindler, S. M. Tipton, *The Good Society*, Vintage, New York, 1992: see also R. N. Bellah (ed), *Postmodern Theology: Christian Faith in a Pluralist World*, Harper, San Francisco, 1989.

Christian resources alone. They are able to do this either because there is a single unambiguously Christian concept – gleaned from the Christian narrative – or because the concept as a whole is simply unChristian. Time-saving as it might be, and popular as it might also be amongst radical postmodern theologians, I have always found such an understanding of Christian ethics to be deeply implausible. Despite the optimism of some of my colleagues, I have yet to be convinced about the adequacy of the links made between the Christian narrative and the resolution of novel moral dilemmas facing the world today.

A much more plausible set of roles for Christian ethics is: firstly to question some moral positions which might otherwise appear logical; secondly to deepen other positions for those of us who have theistic and Christocentric beliefs; and thirdly to point to visions of how things could be if all of humanity was committed to a Christian eschaton. None of these roles is easy. Christian ethics, like moral philosophy, is a profoundly pluralistic discipline and, not surprisingly, Christians disagree amongst themselves about most ethical issues. Divisions on many ethical issues are almost as likely to be found amongst Christian ethicists as amongst other groups of people. Each of these three roles needs to be handled critically.

The first role suggests that some positions, which might appear logical in terms of moral philosophy, are judged by most Christians to be less than Christian. This could be either because they involve unChristian notions or, perhaps more likely, because they are insufficient without other Christian principles or virtues.

Clare Palmer provides clear examples of this towards the end of a philosophical paper on 'Some Problems with Sustainability',[4] where, instructively, she cites positions reached in the World Council of Churches. Taken on its own a notion of sustainable development, or more simply 'sustainability', could be supported by purely totalitarian regimes. Without an accompanying principle of justice, it might be possible to regiment a society in such a way that its future existence was

---

[4] Published in *Studies in Christian Ethics*, Vol. 7, No. 1, pp. 52–62 (parts of my response in *SCE* are incorporated into the present introduction).

assured, even though individuals or minority groups in the meantime were treated unjustly. This, of course, is often seen as the Achilles heel of many versions of utilitarianism: the many survive and prosper, whilst the few unfortunately do not. Without an accompanying (and potentially conflicting) principle of justice it is difficult to avoid this scenario.

Here Christian ethics does have something important to contribute to a general meta-ethical debate. It is a characteristic of most versions of Christian ethics that they do not attempt to reduce everything to a single principle. There have been some (usually short-lived) exceptions – Joseph Fletcher's situation ethics[5] is an obvious example – but for the most part Christian ethicists have been concerned with tensions between principles or values. In contrast, it may be a standing temptation of moral philosophy to reduce ethics to a single principle. There is an understandable, logical elegance involved in such reduction, but most versions of Christian ethics do not function like this. The very resources of Christian ethics – Scripture, tradition and the ever elusive *consensus fidelium* – are far too diverse to allow univocal approaches much credibility.

Thus, most Christian approaches to issues of war and peace have sought some sort of balance between the demands of peace on the one hand and those of justice on the other.[6] For most Christians a concern for peace without an accompanying concern for justice would be inadequate. A long-standing, world dictatorship might be very successful in bringing peace to the world, but it would be much more questionable in terms of justice. Likewise a concern for justice which was indifferent to peace would appear inadequate in most forms of Christian ethics. A tension between justice and peace has, for example, been a continuous tension in liberation theology. A key issue has long been whether liberation can be achieved through non-violent direct action alone or through a contained use of violence. Few, if any, liberation theologians (the most justice oriented of recent Christian ethicists) have been indifferent to the demands of peace.

[5] Joseph Fletcher, *Situation Ethics*, SCM Press, London, 1963.
[6] See further my *A Textbook of Christian Ethics*, T&T Clark, Edinburgh, 1995 (revised edition).

Or, to take another example, at present (especially in the United States) there is considerable stress upon autonomy as a key ethical principle. At times the concept of patient autonomy becomes the single guiding principle to resolve some moral dilemmas in medicine. The pro-choice abortion lobby use it constantly and it is also entering the voluntary euthanasia debate. It is used by some at a macro level to justify the workings of capitalism and/or market forces. The abiding moral virtue of the market place, so it is argued, is that it ensures individual autonomy. Whereas command economies considerably reduce individual autonomy, capitalist economies enhance autonomy. I suspect that most Christian ethicists will regard such claims with suspicion. Even those Christians who are on the economic right or those who are on the medical left (it is ironic that both of these groups tend to use the concept of autonomy in their own area but despise it in the other area) usually temper their claims with some notion of justice or social responsibility. Thus most Christians who are pro-abortion or pro-voluntary euthanasia are also concerned about the implications this might have for the doctors and nurses involved or for society at large. And even those who are most enthusiastic about the moral virtue of market forces tend also to believe that business ethics are still relevant. In short, univocal approaches to ethics are usually regarded as inadequate by those Christians who have given much thought to the subject.

The second role suggests that Christian ethics can seek to deepen moral positions. Naturally this function is dependent upon the theistic and even christological assumptions made by Christians. In theory, if these assumptions are not shared by others, then it is unlikely that they will see this as a helpful role at all. Although, even then, it is possible that theists from a variety of religious traditions may increasingly find common ethical ground – especially if they view the rest of society as purely secular. In practice, Britain still appears to be a society permeated by Christian assumptions and half-beliefs, so this role may yet be considered legitimate beyond the bounds of the churches. For my part, and despite being stimulated by theologians such as Lindbeck or Hauerwas, I shall argue later that it is too early to build the barricades and construct a counter-cultural Christian ghetto. In a pluralistic, postmodern society (rather than a purely secular society) it may be more important than ever for Christians to be articulating ethical issues in distinctively Christian but not exclusive ways – for the benefit of Christians, half-Christians and non-Christians alike – in fact, for the benefit of anyone who will listen.

One of the key differences between Christians (and theists generally) on the one hand and secularists on the other is likely to surround a notion of creation. A notion of sustainability is grounded differently if you believe that the world is created by a loving God than if you do not. The secularist may well resort to one-world rhetoric: 'We have only one life and only one world, so it is up to us to ensure its survival.' The Christian, in contrast, is likely to feel uncomfortable with such rhetoric. Some believe that our comparative destruction of the natural order has resulted precisely from a belief that this life is merely a prelude to something better. Be this as it may, Christian ethicists are likely to talk about the world as a gift rather than as an end in itself. Creation is seen as the gift of a loving Creator and, like most gifts, it should evoke in us a sense of gratitude and responsibility.

Once such theological notions might have been understood as applying simply to human life. It is human beings, not other animals or plants, who are created in the image of the Creator. Under the tutelage of green versions of theology we are learning to be more careful about such claims. Some would interpret this simply as Christians being led by the agenda of the secular world. I would regard it as more complex than that. Christians inevitably respond to each *saeculum*, since we are enjoined to live within the world, and our rich resources of Scripture and tradition offer us insights which can indeed be applied to any *saeculum*. Some *saecula* will be more apposite for these resources than others – and no *saeculum* should be taken as the definitive *saeculum* by any Christian with a sense of Christian history. Yet all *saecula* can be moulded and shaped by these Christian resources. I see green or ecological theology as currently involved in this very task.

The third role for Christian ethics involves the attempt to construct visions of how things could be if all of humanity was committed to a Christian eschaton. This is much the riskiest role, but it is one that has an important history in Christian ethics. The role of the charismatic prophet runs deeply into Christian and Jewish history. The individual who can see through the clutter of presumptions and prejudices of the present *saeculum* and can point to how thing could be if only people would repent and turn back to God. 'Thus saith the Lord.'

I have never been convinced that this is a role for church committees or even, very often, for church leaders.[7] They are typically far too bound up with their surrounding *saeculum* to have the independent vision which is necessary for this role. Even someone of the immense stature of Reinhold Niebuhr was not immune to the prejudices of his times. Established orders are always adept at taming the would-be prophet. The independent critic becomes a part of the establishment – whether in politics, the churches, the universities, or the media – and is typically domesticated in the process. A Reinhold Niebuhr or a Paul Ramsey were both seduced by the validity of American action in Korea or Vietnam. In the early 1980s I was convinced that too many church leaders and theologians in Britain were seduced by the nuclear defence establishment.[8] The mechanisms of power in each *saeculum* are consistently seductive.

Nevertheless, whilst they still remain undomesticated, we are beginning to hear dissonant Christian voices concerned about the environment and the place of future generations of human beings within this environment. Many of us in the North are far too compromised by our cars and labour-devouring gadgets to be serious critics of unsustainable uses of natural resources. I take all the complexities involved in deciding about exactly which natural resources really are irreplaceable or unsubstitutable. Yet whatever the potential fruits of biotechnology, at least according to our present knowledge, those of us who live in the North do seem to be

---

[7] See further my *Prophecy and Praxis*, Marshall, Morgan & Scott, London, 1981.
[8] See further my *The Cross Against the Bomb*, Epworth Press, London, 1984.

committed to a path of unsustainable use. As a result we scarcely make the most independent or credible of critics.

Yet I am heartened by growing voices from the South which see a need to link a concern for political liberation with a concern for environmental protection. In India, for example, I am aware of local theologians voicing increasing concern about the environment – arguing that it is the poor in India who are often the main victims of pollution and environmental degradation.[9] Doubtless the wealthy and articulate throughout the world make effective critics of the destruction of rain forests, the extinction of animals and plants, the pollution of rivers and lakes, and the building of new motorways and railways in previously unspoiled countryside. The inarticulate poor simply have to live with these things. All the more important for local Christians to be acting as prophetic voices in protest.

I am also heartened by the ethical debate that is beginning to emerge amongst biotechnologists, which questions the wisdom of assuming that everything which can be done technologically must be done. There is growing concern that clinical trials in gene therapy may become instead experiments in germ line therapy. Later chapters will attempt to provide a broad ethical map in this new and complex area. If ever there is an area of purely human activity which has the potential to affect future generations (perhaps to the end of human time) it is germ line therapy. In a sense each of us who propagates has some effect on the future of humanity. Yet by altering the germ line, should that become possible, we might be introducing massive changes whose repercussions will be largely unknown to us whilst we are making them. For the most compassionate of reasons – for example, the desire to eliminate fatal hereditary defects either in particular families or even in the human gene pool, which ironically modern medicine otherwise increasingly pollutes – we may introduce disastrous side-effects which will be inherited for generations to come. It is, I believe, a sign of real maturity within the scientific world that such ethical issues are beginning actively to be discussed. For once, they are being discussed

[9] cf. George Mathew, *Towards an Ecotheology for India*, unpublished PhD thesis, University of Kent at Canterbury, December 1995.

before the technology has been developed to allow such environmental changes to happen.

Christian ethics is, I believe, committed to a vision which is ultimately other directed. We are enjoined to love both the Lord our God and our neighbour as ourself. If some versions of moral philosophy are finally concerned only about self-regarding interest, Christian ethics is inescapably altruistic. We should never ignore the other – whether this is our impoverished neighbour now or our children's children's children yet to be born. Religious communities are always committed to some reality beyond themselves and, in the case of the ancient theistic faiths of Judaism, Christianity and Islam, to worship wherein morality is identified in objective terms as not simply our will but God's will. Worship also offers a hope of grace, repentance and forgiveness. Indeed, I shall argue that theistic communities offer stronger grounds for believing in moral order than secular communities: the theist is committed to both physical and moral order, as the natural by-products of a world that is created by a loving God, in a way that tends to be problematic for the atheist. For Christians, in particular, God's loving action in creation and in Christ becomes the very basis of our understanding of moral order.

All of the chapters in this book struggle with these issues that connect faith and moral leadership in the context of an increasingly fragmented and relativistic world – a condition that many depict as 'postmodernity'. In an earlier collection, *Christian Ethics in Secular Worlds*, I brought together studies in three areas: methodology, the environment and society. Some of these interests have been continued here; however a new section has been added on the key issue of the family and postmodernity. In this new book all of the chapters included have been written since the publication of that earlier collection.

Part 1 of this new collection returns once again to issues of method. The first chapter in this section takes a broad look at the implications of postmodernity for church leadership. It was first given in 1996 as a lecture in Uppsala to church leaders, discussed in a seminar at the University of Uppsala, and then delivered again two months later at the University of Auckland.

I am most grateful to theologians and church leaders in both places for helping to shape my ideas. The next chapter, 'Beyond Self-interest', was first given in 1993 as a special lecture to a mixed academic audience at the University of New South Wales, Sydney. The third was given in the following year to a meeting of the Society for the Study of Christian Ethics at Oxford. In all three I seek to address the question of what it is that makes Christian ethics distinctive in a postmodern world. This theme is continued in the fourth chapter, an extended review of Robin Lovin's very useful *Reinhold Niebuhr and Christian Realism*, which I first gave at a Christian ethics symposium at Christ Church, Oxford, in 1995. Lovin's book successfully shows that Niebuhr's concept of Christian realism, despite some obvious weaknesses, does struggle with the issue of Christian distinctiveness whilst remaining fully aware of frailties both in the churches and in the secular world.

Part 2 considers the issues of faith, the family and post-modernity. It opens with a chapter, 'The Changing Family and the Churches', which I first gave at the Society for the Study of Christian Ethics in 1995 and which was subsequently published in *Theology*. This is partly a response to the much debated Anglican report *Something to Celebrate*. However it also seeks to go beyond this report and to ask specifically if there are theological resources that might be used as a rather firmer basis for Christian moral judgments in the vexed areas of sexuality and the family. The two short papers that follow are responses to the seminal papal encyclicals *Veritatis Splendor* and *Evangelium Vitae*. Pope John-Paul II threw down a major challenge both to the churches and to the world at large with these encyclicals. Writing very much as an Anglican, I attempt to set out a positive but critical reaction to them. Following them is a review of Jonathan Sacks' fascinating collection *Faith in the Future*. As an orthodox Jew he is able to set out the dependency of morality on faith, especially on issues concerning the family, rather better than most Christians.

The final part examines a number of emerging and highly contentious moral issues. As society simultaneously becomes more fragmented and more scientifically complex, so moral leaders face ever more difficult issues. In this section I set out, and sometimes just sketch, some of these issues which appear perplexing in a postmodern age. This part of the collection opens with an examination of values in church management. The chapter reflects upon the joint book that I did with Derek Burke, *Strategic Church Leadership*,[10] and was given at the British Sociological Association's Sociology of Religion Study Group in 1996. Two sets of briefing chapters follow. An important role for a Christian ethicist can be to brief church leaders, who otherwise would not have the time to immerse themselves in complex moral issues, but yet who are expected to offer judgments in public. A part of my life is spent doing exactly that: hence the briefing papers. The first is concerned with the emotionally charged area of euthanasia. How should church leaders respond to a growing public pressure for legislation in this area? The next set of briefing papers is in the area of biotechnology. There is a growing public awareness that there are important moral issues at stake here, especially on questions about modifying human beings as a result of IVF and biotechnology. The final chapter considers some of the issues that arise within religious education as a result of both post-modernity and globalisation. Commissioned in 1994 for another collection, on religious education, it seeks to set out some of the tensions arising here from very different under-standings of society.

---

[10] SPCK, London, 1996.

# PART I

# MORALITY
# AND
# POSTMODERNITY

# I

# *Postmodernity and Church Leadership*

If culture is becoming increasingly postmodern, what implications does this have for church leadership on moral issues?
The conditional clause at the beginning of this question itself
raises many questions: Whose culture is it that is becoming
increasingly postmodern? Is it the culture of everyone or that of
the wealthy North rather than the poor South? Or is it just the
culture of educated (perhaps even over-educated) elites within
the North? What is meant by postmodernity? Does postmodernity totally replace modernity? Can postmodernity and
modernity co-exist? Or is postmodernity simply a temporary
regression from a dominant and ongoing modernity? And, if all
of these questions can be answered, why should any of this have
any implications for church leadership? Do church leaders really
have to bother themselves with questions about high culture at
all?

Rather than attempting to give generalised answers to all of
these difficult questions, I propose instead in this chapter to
focus upon a single area, namely medical ethics. Chapters that
follow will attempt to look at other aspects, however a wider
perspective is found in the various monographs[1] that have
appeared in the series *New Studies in Christian Ethics* that I edit
for Cambridge University Press. These are indeed large

---

[1] See especially Ian Markham's *Plurality and Christian Ethics* (1994), James Mackey's
*Power and Christian Ethics* (1994), Jean Porter's *Moral Action and Christian Ethics*
(1995), William Schweiker's *Responsibility and Christian Ethics* (1995), Lisa Sowle
Cahill's *Sex, Gender and Christian Ethics* (1996) and Susan Parsons' *Feminism and
Christian Ethics* (1996): all CUP, Cambridge and New York.

questions which raise fundamental issues within modern theology, especially about the relationship of theology to culture. What unites the studies in the Cambridge series is that all of the contributors agreed to take a key concept of present-day culture very seriously, to be thoroughly familiar with the secular literature on this concept, and yet to explore whether Christian ethics has something distinctive to say about it, either in terms of moral substance or, perhaps more likely, in terms of underlying moral justifications.

Despite cultural pluralism it still seems to be widely assumed that church leaders should offer moral guidance in the area of medical ethics. Whereas their views often seem to be resented by politicians on economic or social policy issues, it does still appear acceptable that church leaders should speak out on issues such as euthanasia, biotechnology, or professional codes of behaviour. As with issues such as sexuality and the family, it does seem to be widely accepted that church leaders should have, and should be prepared to articulate in public, their moral views – even when these views clash with those of others in society. Moral leadership, in these areas at least, is still identified as an appropriate role for church leaders . . . even in a pluralistic or postmodern culture. But what does this entail? And how might church leadership on issues of medical ethics differ in a context of postmodernity from that in a context of modernity?

The outline of an answer to this last question is clear. A generation ago it was widely assumed that medical ethics and Christian ethics were one and the same thing. Many of the earliest exponents of medical ethics were Christian ethicists. In Britain the theologian Alastair Campbell was the first editor of the *Journal of Medical Ethics* and has subsequently become the first Professor of Bioethics both at Otago University and now at Bristol University. Earlier still it was people like Norman Autton in Britain and Joseph Fletcher in the United States – both of them at one time hospital chaplains – who were pioneers of medical ethics. Their books of thirty or more years ago carry many references to the Bible and to Christian literature. Today, however, writings in medical ethics are more distinctly secular in tone. Even when a major contributor is an expert in Christian ethics – such as James Childress in the United States

– or is known to have very committed Christian views – such as Kenneth Calman in Britain – their writings in medical ethics give little indication of this. Furthermore, Alastair Campbell was followed by a secular doctor, Raanon Gillon, as editor of the *Journal of Medical Ethics*, and some of Britain's leading exponents of the discipline, such as Ian Kennedy and John Harris, see themselves as explicitly secular. Nevertheless, medically informed church leaders in Britain, such as the now retired Archbishop of York, John Habgood, are still given considerable space in public to articulate their views on medical ethics. Habgood was even chosen to serve on the House of Lords' Select Committee which considered the vexed question of euthanasia[2] (which will be examined in chapter 10).

Behind this example lies one of the most obvious features of a shift from modernity to postmodernity – namely cultural *fragmentation*. Those whose understanding of postmodernity is largely drawn from literary and critical sources tend to see this fragmentation as a product of what Lyotard called *an incredulity towards meta-narratives*. The notion of secular, rational progress implicit in much of the Enlightenment tradition has become increasingly implausible. In addition, more ancient assumptions that European countries are fundamentally Christian in ethos have also become implausible. No single meta-narrative can hope to secure consensus in a postmodern culture. Both secular rationalism and Christian belief are now seen as faith positions held variously by individuals who lack any common meta-position. Ethics and rationality more generally have effectively now become *privatised*.

Those whose understanding is drawn rather from the physical arts, especially architecture, tend to see postmodernity as a move towards greater *eclecticism*. Modernity represented a break from the old and an advance to some new form: postmodernity abandons this advance and treats all forms as options. In terms of postmodernity, older forms are set alongside newer forms in a move away from some modernist hegemony. If modernity acted like a combine harvester

---

[2] *Report on Medical Ethics*, House of Lords Select Committee Report, HMSO, January 1994.

sweeping away the old crop and transforming it into uniformly square bales, postmodernity allows some of the crop to survive and even to be replanted amidst the bales.[3] In architecture (and fashion) this greater eclecticism has encouraged a jumble of styles set alongside each other – many echoing themes from the past, albeit constructed from materials from the present. At an ethical level it has encouraged a pastiche of disparate voices without any single dominant voice. Thus, the Archbishop of York sat amongst his secular peers on the House of Lord's Select Committee in order to recommend policy to an increasingly confused nation.

Fragmentation, incredulity about meta-narratives, privatisation and eclecticism are all variously seen as features of postmodernity. Added together they are often seen as inducing a strong sense of *moral relativism*. From a literary perspective this moral relativism is again related to an incredulity towards meta-narratives (despite Lyotard's own high moral intentions in challenging the hegemony of scientific explanations). If there are no meta-narratives, there is unlikely to be a common understanding of meta-ethics. So even when people today are largely united in their response to a particular medical ethical issue – with most people, for example, agreeing that it is wrong for patients in the North to buy organs from living donors in the South – they are likely to come to this conclusion from very different premises. Those who are strong theists might broadly agree that all people are created in the image of God and therefore should not be exploited as commodities. However those who are non-theists, or perhaps just weak theists, are unlikely to find this argument very convincing. They might argue instead on the grounds of human rights, of natural justice in a context of unequal power, or even of social prudence (it is bad manners to buy organs from the poor!). And to make matters even more relative, a few philosophers have even justified such sales, arguing that individual enterprise should be allowed if some from the South wish to sell their organs, say, to support their poor families.

---

[3] cf. David Harvey, *The Condition of Postmodernity*, Blackwell, Oxford, 1989: see also Steven Connor, *Postmodernist Culture*, Blackwell, Oxford, 1989.

Relativism of a rather different sort is likely to be identified by those who derive their understanding of postmodernity from the physical arts. Faced with an ever-increasing variety of styles, interpretations and borrowings from the past, there is a growing scepticism that any of them can be regarded as 'authentic' or definitive. To take an obvious example, the early music movement has gone through a number of stages. Two decades ago it was common to hear the expression 'authentic music' or, more accurately, 'music played on authentic instruments'. But, as the movement has become more sophisticated, the difficulties of ever returning to music as it would have been heard in say the eighteenth century have become more apparent. Do we really know how the instruments were played then? Can we be sure that even then there was a single way of playing? What about the extempore playing that was common in the eighteenth century? How is that to be replicated? What about speed, pitch, temperament and dynamics? And, in any case, many composers then used the most avant garde instruments of their time, so is returning to earlier styles of instrument actually in keeping with their own practices? Increasingly 'authentic' has given way to 'variety' and all styles of making music are viewed in relative terms simply as 'options'.

In such a situation of postmodernity how is moral leadership still possible? Clearly it cannot be based upon consensus. If a previous generation of church leaders regarded consensus and the avoidance of conflict as crucial for good leadership, then perhaps a present generation will have to learn otherwise. Church leaders in a postmodern context – whether this context is understood in terms of either the literary approach or that of the physical arts – can no longer assume a common framework within which consensus is possible. This may apply to church leadership both within the churches and in society at large. Plurality is writ large into the postmodern condition.

In *Strategic Church Leadership*,[4] which I recently wrote with Derek Burke, we argue that there has been a move away from consensus in many arenas. For example, leadership in British universities has undergone a dramatic transformation over the

[4] SPCK, London, 1996.

last two decades – moving from consensual leadership and incremental budgeting to strategic planning, budgeting, implementation and audit. However, leadership in most British churches has yet to make this transition. Church leaders typically proceed on the basis of consensus and carrying forward historic budgets from one year to the next, with financial cuts when they are required by declining income made evenly and without clear, limited and audited objectives. Indeed, there is often strong resistance amongst church leaders and clergy alike to any move away from consensus, especially from consensus based upon clerical autonomy, or from even-handed, incremental budgeting – often on the assumption that 'secular' management and leadership concepts are at best irrelevant, or at worst inimical, to the churches (here too, these assumptions will be examined in detail in the final section).

In contrast, we claim in *Strategic Church Leadership* that church leaders do already have implicit styles of management and leadership and that, compared with many other similar organisations, these implicit styles are now widely regarded as anachronistic. Consensus management, clerical autonomy and incremental budgeting are often deemed preferable in churches to strategic understandings of leadership and to new forms of management based upon priorities and accountability. In contrast, we argue that consensus styles of management are often both ineffective and flawed. Morally they are flawed because they tend to give (usually clerical) minorities a powerful veto to thwart the will of the majority. This has been a recurrent experience since the introduction of synodical government in the Church of England. Logistically they are flawed because organisations committed to consensus can only change on the basis of common ground which might actually be peripheral to all the parties concerned. The moral flaw will be examined later: the logistical flaw can be set out now.

The Decade of Evangelism provides an instructive example of this logistical flaw. Provided that 'evangelism' or 'mission' are defined in the most general terms there is a widespread agreement amongst Anglican clergy (and doubtless also amongst Free Church ministers) that they are desirable. It is not too difficult to get consensus for such propositions as 'the Christian faith is relevant to the whole of life' or 'the parochial system of the Church of England is designed to be available to the whole population of England'. These are important points, but they do not generate agreed strategies. It is possible to hold such propositions and still believe that the number of people coming to church is irrelevant: it is enough for church buildings and their clergy to be available in every locality whether or not the local population makes any tangible use of them. Confronted with statistics of churchgoing decline,[5] it is possible to adopt quite opposite strategies whilst still affirming the two consensus propositions. One common reaction is to deny the empirical evidence, the basis upon which it has been gathered, or the degree to which it is uninterrupted. Another reaction is to deny that statistics are relevant at all and another again is to say that strategies are urgently needed to counter this process. Unfortunately all of these reactions seem to be prevalent amongst Anglican clergy, so it may not be too surprising that it is only approximately a third of parishes that have shown a numerical increase in churchgoing during the Decade of Evangelism (or 'Evangelisation' for Roman Catholics). By definition two-thirds have not, so at the end of the Decade it is possible that in most identifiable indices Anglicans will still be in decline.

A similar pattern can be detected in the moral leadership of many church leaders. Assuming Britain to be still fundamentally Christian, church leaders in a previous generation could presume that there was a broad moral consensus in Britain based upon abiding Christian principles. William Temple's classic *Christianity and Social Order* is an obvious example of this approach. A much respected Archbishop could arbitrate on social and moral issues for the nation on the basis of shared Christian principles. He expected to be corrected on technical details when making an ethical decision, but not on these principles. This led him to his famous claim that the church acting corporately could set principles for the nation whilst not committing itself to particular political policies. For

[5] In *The Myth of the Empty Church*, SPCK, London, 1993, I show that there has been an uninterrupted process of urban Anglican decline since the 1850s.

him the problem was that 'a policy always depends on technical decisions concerning the actual relation of cause and effect in the political and economic world; about these a Christian as such has no more reliable judgement than an atheist, except so far as he should be more immune to the temptations of self-interest'.[6] Even his own detailed political programme he assigned to an appendix of *Christianity and Social Order*, adding impishly that 'if any member of the Convocation of York should be so ill-advised as to table a resolution that these proposals be adopted as a political programme for the church, I should in my capacity as Archbishop resist that proposal with all my force, and should probably, as President of the Convocation, rule it out of order'.[7] However, what the church should do corporately, he argued, is identify and defend the key moral principles that ought to form the basis of political decision-making in the nation. On these principles there could be a consensus between church and nation.

It is possible that this approach was always based upon an idealised understanding of society (and probably of the churches too), even of British society in the early 1940s. Immigration from the Caribbean, from Asia and from Africa was yet to introduce the rich mixture of ethnic and religious groups apparent in Britain today. But there had already been substantial groups of immigrant Jews and there had been a long-established pattern of religious dissent, of low churchgoing especially in many urban and rural deprived areas, and even of overt secularism. If Britain, or more accurately, England, appeared to be culturally uniform in the 1940s, this appearance may have owed more to a hegemony amongst its leaders than to a uniformity in the population itself. William Temple had, after all, been to school and university with many of the most senior politicians, civil servants and academics of his time. It was *they* who shared a common culture, not necessarily the population at large. So perhaps the features of postmodernity were present amongst the people long before the concept became common currency amongst the governing and intellectual elite. Today,

---

[6] William Temple, *Christianity and Social Order*, Penguin, London, 1942, pp. 27–8.
[7] ibid., pp. 28–9.

however, even this elite has changed – members of the governing and intellectual elite, and even Anglican Archbishops, are no longer 'reliably' drawn in England from a single social class (in Scotland they never were).

The problem of the church leader in a postmodern, or perhaps just pluralist, society is how to offer moral leadership without being able to presume a common moral framework. In medical ethics this problem is increasingly resolved, or at least shelved, by agreeing to a set of *bridging principles*. It is worth noting that medical ethics is a form of professional ethics which is already far more mature than most other forms of professional ethics, including those in both universities and churches (surprisingly, clergy seldom have a written code of professional ethics). So perhaps the current uneasy truce in medical ethics is worth observing. It might offer a clue to effective church leadership in this area.

An example can be taken from the work of ethics committees which have now become mandatory in areas of medical research in Britain. Whilst there is a widespread realisation that many research projects do raise ethical issues, there is much confusion about how these issues might be resolved. A common experience in ethics committees monitoring research is that it is difficult to move beyond individual opinion. People do not agree with each other about how they derive and justify their ethical beliefs. So each member of an ethics committee seems to be in danger simply of importing particular beliefs or prejudices without any agreed common criteria. Much then depends upon who is or is not selected to serve on an ethics committee in the first place. Are certain political, ideological or religious groups to be excluded? Is it right or even possible to get a 'balanced' committee? Does the committee represent 'common' experience or rather 'educated' experience? Thus, questions of selection become dominant rather than agreed ethical criteria.

It was partly for this reason that in medical ethics it was thought important to identify certain broad principles which might be agreed upon by otherwise divergent groups. The four principles that are now widely accepted are: **non-maleficence**, **beneficence**, **autonomy** and **justice**. There is still much debate about exactly how these four principles are to be balanced and about how they might be justified.[8] Nevertheless in medical ethics it is now widely recognised that they should all be taken into consideration when considering particular ethical issues:

**Non-maleficence** suggests that a proposed research project should not cause harm. For example, research projects seeking to interview child abusers face particularly difficult problems since they may uncover evidence which incriminates those being interviewed. Other research projects might risk physical danger. For example, there has been much discussion amongst biotechnologists about the potential risks of genetic release, that is, about the danger of genetically changed organisms escaping or being released into the environment.

**Beneficence** suggests that research projects, especially those involving people or higher animals, should strive positively to bring benefit. Even if no harm is being done, good research should still aim to benefit people, animals, or perhaps the environment. So research upon people or higher animals which has no clear objectives about benefit, but which is simply undertaken out of curiosity, would be difficult for an ethics committee to support. Such a committee would be looking for some positive indications of benefit.

**Autonomy** suggests that when research projects involve people then they should be treated with respect, they should be informed adequately, and they should give their consent without coercion. In short people should be treated as people and not simply as research objects. Informed consent causes many problems in research projects: some projects are so complex that it is difficult to get properly *informed* consent. For example, the genome project is showing just how complicated human genetic inheritance is. Would any programme of widespread genetic screening be able adequately to inform all those taking part? (Again, the third part will return to this issue.) And what about research on those with severe learning disabilities? How does one properly gain informed consent from this group of people? Clearly, in a society which is increasingly educated, informed consent and respect for the autonomy of people are important. Whatever the difficulties,

[8] See Raanon Gillon (ed), *Principles of Health Care Ethics*, Wiley, Chichester, 1994.

it is maintained that research projects should take this fully into consideration.

**Justice** suggests that research projects should always take into consideration the concerns of the whole of society and should be particularly vigilant about minority groups that might be disadvantaged by the research. The relative distribution of resources for research projects is often contentious for this reason. Should large amounts of money be used for research on HIV/AIDS, which involves a small number of people, or upon heart disease, which involves many more? Will some research projects benefit people in relatively affluent countries to the disadvantage of those in the poorest countries? Such question have sometimes been raised about research projects on genetically improved food resources. Do these resources finally disadvantage the poorest nations which become even more dependent upon rich countries' patents, products and even fertilisers? At a global level, questions of justice also involve environmental questions. For example, genetically improved resources might have an adverse effect upon ecological balances and biodiversity.

It should be stressed that in medical ethics these are essentially *bridging principles*. They represent a general, but perhaps just temporary, truce amongst different groups that have an interest in medical ethics. People with differing political, ideological and religious beliefs will no doubt give quite different and even conflicting reasons for supporting them: there is no presumption of a common meta-ethic. They may even understand them and the balance between them differently. Yet many might still agree that all four principles can be used with benefit both in ethics committees and in medical ethics more generally. They seek to provide common ground for otherwise diverse groups of people in a pluralist, postmodern society.

But do they offer church leaders an adequate framework for moral leadership in a postmodern age? Well, they might, but they are still more than a little fragile. The position and status of the third principle, that of individual 'autonomy', illustrates this well. The relative status given to individual autonomy has a profound effect upon medical ethics. From a perspective of

Christian ethics this can be disturbing. Instead of ethics being 'other directed', it can instead soon become an egoistic claim to individual 'rights' and 'entitlements': self-giving is replaced by a list of demands. The adequacy for Christian ethics of the principle of 'autonomy' will be tested in several of the chapters that follow. It will be seen that Pope John-Paul II's encyclical *Veritatis Splendor* makes some sharp observations about the limitations of 'autonomy' as it often appears in secular culture, wherein individual choice becomes the hallmark of postmodern morality, yet individual choice is apparently no longer possible. A secular morality demands individual choice, whereas much secular social science apparently denies that it is even possible. All we seem to be left with is a rather bleak and despairing relativism.

Stanley Hauerwas has made a speciality out of parodying such secular forms of ethics. His writings increasingly represent a radical postmodern response to ethics, as the title of one his recent books indicates starkly, namely *Resident Aliens.*[9] Christian ethics is wholly different from secular ethics and Christians finally have no business in trying to pretend that things are otherwise. His advice to church leaders seems to be that they must eschew forms of medical ethics which are anything less than explicitly Christian. The discipline of Christian ethics is based upon the formation of character within the context of Christian communities; it is not the business of proponents of this discipline to engage in discussions about *bridging principles* with secular medicine. In a morally confused world, Christians will appear increasingly like 'resident aliens'; they should not seek to compromise with this world. It is their role to preach and to witness against it and to let their lives be shaped wholly by the Christian narrative. If meta-narratives have collapsed, then it becomes even more important that Christians learn to understand and articulate the distinctiveness of their own narrative. Finally, it is from this narrative that true Christian virtues are to be derived. It is these virtues and not the Enlightenment principles of autonomy and non-maleficence that offer the true path for Christians.

[9] Abingdon Press, Nashville, 1989.

This almost sounds like a parody of Hauerwas, but it is actually quite difficult to parody him. As his fame has increased, so his rhetoric has also increased. Even ten years ago, in what is arguably one of his best books, *Suffering Presence: Theological Reflections on Medicine, the Mentally Handicapped, and the Church* (the phrase 'mentally handicapped' shows its vintage), he argued:

> In this book I argue that the rise of 'medical ethics' is due more to the confused moral world we inhabit than to our technological revolution. 'Medical ethics' therefore does not so much solve our difficulties as it reflects the moral anarchy of our times, for it is by no means clear how the practice of medicine can be sustained in a morally fragmented society. Put more strongly, it is by no means clear in such a society what the practice of medicine is about. Modern medicine's desperate attempt to cure through increasing use of technology may be but a way of avoiding the fact that it lacks any moral rationale for dealing with death's inevitability.[10]

Yet, having made such a claim, one suspects that Hauerwas, like the rest of us, still goes to his doctor when he feels ill – whether the doctor is a Christian or not. He may even ask for the benefits of the latest form of medical technology. As so often in his writings – immensely stimulating as they are – there seems to be an extraordinary gap between theory and practice. The world may not be quite as confused as he claims, nor may the churches be quite as pure as he might hope. If the confusions of postmodernity affect both church and world, the bridging points between church and world may ensure that there is still a place for a Christian ethicist even within an apparently secular world.

Nevertheless there are a number of important ways in which religious communities tend to differ from secular communities. The three ways sketched in the introduction are particularly important. Each of them suggests that the connection between religious faith and morality may be rather stronger than is

[10] Stanley Hauerwas, *Suffering Presence*, University of Notre Dame Press, Ind., 1986, and T&T Clark, Edinburgh, 1988, pp. 1–2.

sometimes imagined; each also offers a path that church leaders might pursue further even in a context of postmodernity:

The first of these relates to tradition. The ancient religions are all carriers of values and traditions which have been tested and refined over time. Sometimes this makes church leaders seem hesitant and even old-fashioned in fast-changing times. Bishops in the Church of England, for example, are currently struggling with the issues of divorce and homosexuality. It would be easy for them simply to go along with surrounding culture in the West and treat all sexual issues as simply a matter of private opinion (personal autonomy and mutual consent are rapidly becoming the only public standards in this area).[11] But leaders of a religious community that has been around for a long time are likely to be more circumspect. Their community has seen fashions change before and is wary of simply being swept along by the latest tide. For most religious communities sexuality is also about responsibility and about building up a caring and considerate society which protects and sustains its own children. 'Faithfulness' rather than 'autonomy' becomes crucial in this context (a chapter in the next section will consider this further).

As carriers of ancient and refined moral wisdom, religious communities have few rivals today. However, in a postmodern world religious communities may find that their refined moral wisdom comes under increasing attack from determined secularists. The writings of the Australian philosopher Peter Singer over the last decade illustrate this clearly. His recent book *Rethinking Life and Death* has the instructive subtitle *The Collapse of Our Traditional Ethics*. Using a number of current legal judgments about the withdrawal of nutrition and hydration from persistent vegetative state patients and the increasing *de facto* acceptance of more direct forms of euthanasia as his starting point, he offers a sustained polemic against what he sees as the collapsing Judaeo-Christian ethical tradition. If Stanley Hauerwas is the *enfant terrible* of Christian ethics, then Peter Singer is fast becoming the *enfant terrible* of secular ethics.

[11] cf. Lisa Sowle Cahill, *Sex, Gender and Christian Ethics*, CUP, New York and Cambridge, 1996.

For the latter ancient and refined moral wisdom is to be replaced by individual self-awareness and rationality, allowing him astonishingly to justify infanticide. He argues:

> In the modern era of liberal abortion laws, most of those not opposed to abortion have drawn a sharp line at birth. If, as I have argued, that line does not mark a sudden change in the status of the fetus, then there appear to be only two possibilities: oppose abortion, or allow infanticide. I have already given reasons why the fetus is not the kind of being whose life must be protected in the way that the life of a person should be. Although the fetus may, after a certain point, be capable of feeling pain, there is no basis for thinking it rational or self-aware, let alone capable of seeing itself as existing in different times and places. But the same can be said of a newborn infant. Human babies are not born self-aware, or capable of grasping that they exist over time. They are not persons. Hence their lives would seem to be no more worthy of protection than the life of a fetus.[12]

Singer does retreat slightly from this conclusion – after all a baby can no longer be viewed as a part of a woman's body – but only slightly. He does finally believe that infanticide can be ethically justified and is fully aware that this conclusion sharply challenges many forms of religious ethics. Faced with such secularist polemics, religious traditions may appear increasingly distinctive.

Secondly, religious communities are always committed to some reality beyond themselves. Even those forms of religious tradition which have no explicit belief in God still have a commitment to transcendence. At the heart of the ancient theistic faiths of Judaism, Christianity and Islam is worship. In worship we are reminded constantly that 'what is good' relates not simply to our will but to God's will. Morality is seen as objective and not simply subjective. Furthermore in almost every act of worship we are invited to repent and to seek forgiveness. We are offered the opportunity for renewal and absolution. Whereas many secular communities 'know' that they are right and that others are wrong, religious communities

---

[12] Peter Singer, *Rethinking Life and Death*, OUP, Oxford, 1995, p. 210.

encourage their members instead to recognise their own frailty and sinfulness and through that to seek forgiveness. In a secular world that knows much about guilt (just think about all those nature programmes on television telling us constantly about our destruction of the environment) but little about repentance and forgiveness, religious communities instead typically offer both means of repentance and forgiveness and the hope of grace beyond them. As I shall argue later, worship offers a distinctive role for church leaders in a postmodern age.

Thirdly, theistic communities offer stronger grounds for believing in moral order than secular communities. In the late twentieth century we are rather better at noticing moral order in a negative sense than in a positive sense. To put this another way, we are rather better at recognising what is bad than what is good. Most people know that the Holocaust, genocide, child abuse and systematic torture are wrong in some objective sense. From this it follows that those responsible for such appalling evils are usually regarded as moral degenerates or even socio-paths. They cannot properly hide behind the claim that they were simply obeying orders (as was claimed at Nuremberg) or that they did not realise that they were doing wrong. They should have known that such evil acts are wrong and that they express deep moral disorder.

Those of us who believe in a God who created and sustains the world will usually want to add more at this point. For us these acts of appalling evil are not just expressions of deep moral disorder, they are also offences against God's created order. The theist is committed to moral order in a way that is more problematic for the atheist and which may well go beyond the boundaries of thoroughgoing postmodernity. The theist typically believes that both moral order (which is presupposed by objective moral outrage) and physical order (which is pre-supposed by the natural sciences) are the natural by-products of a world that is created by a loving God. Of course, many atheists do still believe in moral order and especially in physical order, but their grounds for such beliefs are less clear. Presumably things just happen fortuitously to be that way rather than in a state of radical disorder. Natural science would soon come to a halt without some such belief. But why should there be moral order? And, even if there is moral order, why should any individual feel obliged to follow it?

Belief in a loving, caring God gives much stronger grounds for a notion of moral order than this. Since church leaders are obviously committed to such a God, they are no longer committed simply to the 'is' – they are just as concerned about the 'could be'. They believe that God will continue to sustain the world, offering people made in the image of God both purpose and moral direction. They are committed to the belief that we should care for others and for the rest of the created order precisely because we believe that God the creator has first cared for us. God's loving action in creation becomes the very basis of our understanding of moral order. Perhaps they could argue that this is so more publicly. In contrast, the secularist position may be rather weaker than is sometime imagined.

All three ways go beyond the four bridging principles currently used in medical ethics but they do not negate them. Provided that autonomy is held in tension with justice, it need not succumb simply to self-interest. Provided that non-maleficence is held in tension with beneficence, it is consonant with the ways of Christian love. Whilst working with and not against these bridging principles, church leaders might argue that their faith offers a more profound and secure basis for them than does a purely secular vision. Indeed the very notion of beneficence presupposes a notion of 'doing good' which has often proved elusive in secular philosophy. Postmodernity fragments but it also challenges faith groups and their leaders to be distinctive. Perhaps the challenge is finally to articulate Christian principles which are distinctive but not exclusive. And that, in a postmodern age, is surely a very proper task for church leadership.

# 2

### ~+☸+~

# *Beyond Self-interest*

Paradoxically, a concern for others which goes beyond self-interest seems essential to most forms of ethics, yet it is frequently argued in a postmodern age that self-interest alone or, perhaps more accurately, self-regarding interest alone, regulates all moral behaviour. Furthermore, in many ethical arguments today notions such as those of autonomy or of individual entitlements and rights are frequently stressed, but only occasionally is it mentioned that people may also have correlative duties and responsibilities. Later chapters will return to the issue of autonomy in relation to Christian ethics, whereas this chapter will focus upon altruism and the problems that it raises. Frequently, altruism is regarded as either impossible or else as an exception reserved for saints, even though most forms of morality soon disintegrate without an element of altruism. To complete the paradox, it appears again and again that behaviour contradicts theory: people apparently do still behave altruistically even when they claim that altruistic behaviour is (at least for ordinary mortals) impossible.

Just imagine for a moment that self-regarding interest really is the only yardstick for moral action. People decide to do something only if they can see that it is in their own interests to do so. Of course, these interests could be long-term interests, even exceedingly long-term interests, but they are nonetheless self-regarding interests. Duty never requires people to say that they will act beyond self-regarding interest. Responsibility to others, in the final analysis, means no more than responsibility to self.

On this understanding, a wife who looks after her husband with Alzheimer's disease ultimately bases her action only upon self-regarding interest. This might be immediate self-interest, since looking after the stricken husband gives her a warm glow of maternal feeling. She derives a strong sense of self-satisfaction from caring for him. It is somewhat like the terrible contortions that Leo Tolstoy managed to entrap himself within. He wanted to be humble and to embody what he saw as peasant virtues, but in reality he was not the slightest bit humble and he was a Russian count not a Russian peasant. When he went on an anonymous pilgrimage he took his footman with him and was soon identified by the monks and given the best guest-chamber. Recounting this story, Stephen Sykes observes: 'Humility so often eludes us. It needs self-forgetfulness (the fruit of a habit of attention to others) and unobtrusiveness (a willingness to be undiscovered).'[1]

Manifestly Tolstoy lacked both of these virtues. The great, perhaps greatest, novelist was unable to walk for more than a mile or two of the pilgrimage wearing peasant clogs. His footman could not resist gloating about this afterwards, whilst observing that it was he who finally produced woollen socks for his master's blistered feet. Tolstoy returned from his pilgrimage by train (third class, of course) to be met at the station by his personal carriage. Altruism defeated by short-term self-interest.

Perhaps it is middle-distance self-interest, so to speak, which governs the woman's behaviour in caring for her husband with Alzheimer's disease. She realises that she may one day be helpless and vulnerable herself and she wishes to ensure that she too, will be cared for in the way that she now cares for the shell that is left of her husband – a sort of John Rawls' calculation.[2] Rather like taking out a life insurance policy, prudence suggests that it is better to be on the safe side. Standing behind a veil of ignorance people can never be too sure that they might not end up amongst the disadvantaged. So in the meantime it is sensible to care for others who are in need as a sort of insurance policy. This is prudential logic based upon middle-distance self-interest

---

[1] Stephen Sykes, 'Hard to Achieve Self-forgetfulness', *Church Times*, 8 April 1993, p. 10.

[2] John Rawls, *A Theory of Justice*, OUP, New York, 1973, p. 136.

and not, as it might at first appear, upon genuine altruism. Or it might even be ultimate self-interest that inspires the woman to care for her afflicted husband. She believes that one day she will be rewarded in heaven for her present actions in caring beyond immediate self-interest.

One way or another it is not difficult to explain, what might at first appear to be altruistic action on the part of the woman caring for her demented husband, instead in terms of nothing but self-regarding interest. Like Count Tolstoy, she appears to be vulnerable to self-interest at every turn.

I believe that such explanations based exclusively upon self-interest are deeply unsatisfactory. They also pay scant regard to accounts given by those who care for stricken spouses. Such explanations might or might not work for someone as self-obsessed as Tolstoy, but they seriously distort understandings of more everyday behaviour. Suspicions might immediately be roused by the fact that in everyday speech people do regularly distinguish between those who are more self-interested than others as in the statements: 'All that person is interested in is himself', or, 'He is the most self-centred person I have ever met.' As the philosopher Charles Taylor insists in his influential book *Sources of the Self*,[3] it is important to pay attention to the assumptions behind ethical discourse as well as to the formal theories or articulations of that discourse.

For example, many will have little difficulty in distinguishing between the moral motivation of the late Gordon Wilson and the moral motivation of those members of the IRA who were responsible for killing his daughter Marie in the Remembrance Day bombing at Enniskillen. In his report of meeting with members of the IRA, the difference between Gordon Wilson's moral stance and their moral stance was pellucid:

> I said there was no excuse for the killing of innocent civilians, including Marie Wilson and the two innocent little children in Warrington and dozens of others . . . They said they do not condone, nor indeed do they set out to kill innocent civilians,

[3] Charles Taylor, *Sources of the Self: The Making of the Modern Identity*, CUP, Boston and Cambridge, 1989.

men, women, or little children. I said: 'I am sorry, I cannot
accept that. You do not convince me, and I cannot accept,
that the bomb you placed in Enniskillen was intended only
for the security forces – which in itself was wrong, in my
opinion. Because you knew that there would be civilians there
and that 99 per cent of the people who were there would be
Protestants' . . . I tried with all the sincerity and honesty and
integrity I could muster to get over my simple request with as
much conviction as I could. They listened, but they made no
change in their position. Perhaps it was naive of me to imagine
that because it was me they would . . . They told me history is
on their side.[4]

The word naive is important in this account. Gordon Wilson
had been widely reported before his meeting with the IRA as
being motivated more by altruism than by pragmatism – but
that in an age of self-interest may simply appear as naiveté. The
IRA members, in contrast, were clear about their own political
demands and were not to be deflected by the pleas of a grieving
father. They had rights and entitlements on their side and were
convinced that their goal of political autonomy was justified
whatever the human cost. Gordon Wilson's plea, in contrast,
was for pity, for mercy and for reconciliation – virtues con-
spicuously missing from the agenda of self-interest.

It would be difficult to make such moral distinctions without
being able also to distinguish between people who are more
self-interested and others who are less self-interested. At the very
least there must be an ability to conceive of people who are
relatively un-self-interested, that is to say people whose centre
of attention is not solely themselves or their particular group.
Of course, it is still possible to hold that Gordon Wilson's
extraordinary and seemingly altruistic behaviour was motivated
by grief. Yet others grieve and they more usually express feelings
of bitterness and retribution. The absence of such public
expressions by Gordon Wilson persistently amazed world-weary
journalists.

It is surprising just how many people fail to spot that moral
judgments, even negative ones, imply standards. Charles Taylor,
in contrast, argues that morality presumes a moral framework

---

[4] *The Independent*, 9 April 1993, p. 2.

and that one's moral framework is intimately connected with one's personal identity. For him, 'my identity is defined by the commitments and identifications which provide the frame or horizon within which I can try to determine from case to case what is good, or valuable, or what ought to be done, or what I endorse or oppose'.[5] Thus, moral outrage, unless it is to be considered to be on a par say with indigestion or bad breath, presupposes some abiding value or set of values. Yet ironically other academics frequently claim that notions of good are entirely relative and/or optional, whilst in the next breath expressing unqualified moral outrage at some deep injustice, which of course they believe everybody else ought to identify as a deep injustice. 'Yes, values are just a matter of passing opinion; and yes, the bombing of civilians whilst at prayer at Enniskillen was deeply wrong.' With one breath people, even intelligent people, seem capable of denying that there are any abiding values in the world (least of all any religiously derived values), whilst regarding Auschwitz as *self-evidently evil.*

Similarly they denounce Christian belief on the grounds of the egregious behaviour of Christians down the centuries – as if abuse was ever a valid criticism of use. Or they denounce the idea of the Christian God for creating such an evil world, whilst using Christian values as the very basis of their denunciations. John Updike captures this irony on the lips of a disillusioned and lecherous priest in his novel *A Month of Sundays.* The priest finds a way to justify his own adultery by denouncing the God to whom he had once committed his life. He compares God unfavourably with the divorced organist he lusts after in his church:

> Precisely, I worshipped her, adored her flaws as furiously as her perfections, for they were hers; and thus I attained, in the bound of a few spring weeks, a few illicit lays, the attitude which saints bear toward God, and which I in a Christ's life-time of trying (40 [present age] minus 7 [age of reason] equals 33) had failed to reach, that is, of forgiving Him the pain of infants, the inexorability of disease, the wantonness of fortune, the billions of fossilised deaths, the helplessness of the

⁵ Taylor, op. cit., p. 27.

young, the idiocy of the old, the craftsmanship of torturers, the authority of blunderers, the savagery of accident, the unbreathability of water, and all the other repulsive flecks on the face of Creation.[6]

Because Updike's fictional character is a priest – albeit a very distorted one (his face on the Penguin edition of the novel is made up of a mass of contorted women's bodies) – the moral outrage apparent in this passage is manifestly a part of his Christian background. This is no secular attack upon religious faith, but a Job-like denunciation of God from within a context of faith. The moral categories that the deeply depressed priest uses are theologically inspired categories. Updike goes to great lengths to demonstrate his own prowess in technical theology and thus to confirm this very point. Yet repeatedly in a postmodern culture similar categories are used to denounce the possibility of faith, as if these categories are themselves purely secular or even justifiable upon purely secular grounds. Belief in a Creator God is univocally denounced as a moral obscenity in the name of a secularity which purportedly believes that all values are relative and that all morality is a matter of individual preference alone.

Another example of this was provided in real life by the extraordinary public reaction to the establishment of a lectureship in theology and natural science at Cambridge University. The endowment for this lectureship was provided by another popular novelist Susan Howatch. It was immediately attacked in a series of letters to *The Independent* newspaper.[7] Chief amongst the critics was the Oxford biologist Richard Dawkins. Author instructively of *The Selfish Gene* and *The Blind Watchmaker*, he denounced the lectureship, asking what science could possibly learn from theology and reminding readers of the many evils that had been committed in the world as a result of religious faith.

Many in the theological world were amazed to find that such scientism was still alive outside the walls of a sixth-form physics class. After all the evident moral dilemmas facing, and perhaps

---

[6] John Updike, *A Month of Sundays*, Penguin, Harmondsworth, 1976, p. 36.
[7] *The Independent*, April 1993.

even caused by, the application of science to an ever more complex world,[8] here was an impassioned defence of faith in science allied to a 'scientific' denunciation of faith in religion. Science was upheld as the only true arbiter of knowledge and theology was impaled in a value-laden critique of religious faith. The irony of combining these two positions may have escaped Richard Dawkins, but it did not escape Susan Howatch. Whilst her novels may not be as theologically penetrating as those of John Updike, she offered a spirited defence of the lectureship she had endowed. To the criticism of the harmonica player Larry Adler (who echoed strongly Richard Dawkins' stance), she simply pointed out that the fact that most other people make dreadful noises on the harmonica does not imply that the harmonica is an unworthy object of interest and study. And, in any case, why had her act of giving away money been the signal for so much public vitriol? If moral outrage is to be expressed in public, she argued, why not reserve it for, say, money spent on acts of cruelty or money hoarded in a needy world?

Of course, self-regarding interest may be a feature of many, perhaps even most, moral actions. There is indeed a proper place for self-regarding interest, since if people lose interest in themselves they may well lose interest in everybody else as well. Self-hatred is a deeply destructive emotion. There is also the important feminist point that it is sometimes assumed too readily that it is women not men who should be altruistic (for this reason some feminists prefer the term 'mutuality'). Yet to view self-regarding interest as the *only* satisfactory explanation of moral behaviour may also be deeply destructive. It effectively destroys most of what is distinctive about moral behaviour.

Faced with the daily indignities and bickerings involved in caring for those they once loved, but who now have Alzheimer's, few report that they get some warm glow of maternal feeling. Perhaps it is possible to ignore the indignities involved in child rearing precisely because parents can see a life that is slowly

[8] cf. Ian Barbour, *Ethics in an Age of Technology: The Gifford Lectures*, Vol. 2, SCM Press, London, 1992.

developing, a person who is emerging. Perhaps it was possible for Count Tolstoy to get a momentary glow of self-satisfaction as he pretended to be the Russian peasant which he palpably was not. After all, he had a vivid imagination and he could always escape back to the privileged world of a nineteenth-century Russian aristocrat whenever he wished. Yet in the case of permanently impaired partners life is slowly, agonisingly slowly, disintegrating, almost submerging. There is nothing much to look forward to, short-term or long-term . . . only the eventual release of death. There is little glow of self-satisfaction there. The long grind of chronic, terminal illness – like the long grind of intractable poverty (as distinct from the elected, and therefore reversible, poverty of Tolstoy ) – is not rich hunting ground for warm glows of any kind.

More frequently partners of those with Alzheimer's disease do talk about their hopes that one day, if they are similarly afflicted, they too will be the recipients of care. But is this an explanation or just a hope? The notion of do-as-you-would-be-done-by, based upon an unspoken since-you-never-know-when-you-might-need-to-be-done-by, may well be important in many consequentialist accounts of ethics. Yet it may not be so convincing to those who are determinedly self-interested. People might take out insurance policies to protect their houses, since these are cheap compared to the loss of a house. And in any case a requirement of taking mortgages is usually that they must be protected by adequate insurance. However, to engage in years of seemingly selfless action simply on the off-chance that they might need it one day themselves seems less than plausible.

Determinedly self-interested people are in reality concerned to get *more* than their fair due, not to give out more than they are ever likely to get back again. For them it is more profitable to ignore those in need now and then to manipulate the consciences of the gullible and naive when they are in need themselves. Thankfully only a handful of people really do act in such a determinedly self-interested way. Yet that in itself might offer a clue that, despite postmodernity, altruism and/ or mutuality are far from absent. Implicitly we depend upon most other people not being determinedly self-interested.

Indeed a society of completely self-interested people would be a nightmare for the vulnerable and needy, especially, but also hardly comfortable for the rest of us. If all are concerned to get more than their 'due', then all but a small minority may end up losers. Instructively, determinedly self-interested people are now labelled 'sociopaths'. The behaviour patterns of many chronic alcoholics unwittingly provide abundant evidence of such behaviour and, in turn, suggest that most people are not like that.

What about the ultimate temptation for religious faith in morality – to regard sacrificial behaviour in this world as an object of reward in the next world? Life may be uncomfortable in this world looking after a confused and complaining spouse, but as a direct result it will be considerably more comfortable in the next. Heavenly rewards compensate for earthly trials – a belief that might aptly be termed eternal self-regarding interest.

In contrast, many religious traditions stress that heavenly bliss cannot be derived from such crude works. Indeed it does seem to be a feature of many religious traditions (theistic as well as Buddhist) that they encourage adherents to move beyond self-interest. A feature that Nietzsche identified (and, of course, vehemently opposed) as being essentially Christian is in reality shared by a number of faiths. An effective relationship to God, or (in Buddhism) the attainment of a state of personal holiness, requires believers to be open and responsive to the 'other'. It requires the faithful to be less concerned with entitlements that are due to themselves or to rights that they might claim and, instead, to be other-regarding. In Christian terms 'not my will, but thy will be done' and not us but 'Christ working in and through us'. The language of grace is anything but self-regarding. More than that, the doctrine of prevenient grace suggests that autonomous, self-regarding ethics is scarcely possible at all. Within this Christian understanding, ethics is seen as both other-regarding and as only made possible by God's grace going before it.

In any case, such a crude theory of eternal rewards is seldom given by those who care for stricken spouses. Overwhelmingly what they mention is 'duty'.[9] They care for those they once loved, so they report, precisely because they feel that it is their duty to do so. Whether or not feelings of love survive the degradations of Alzheimer's, they still feel a deep sense of responsibility. If the languages of duty and responsibility survive anywhere in a self-regarding culture, it is surely here.

Ironically, the elderly caring for stricken spouses are frequently told to give up by the young. The repeated phrase that any family doctor will have heard dozens of times from the children of such couples is 'Doctor, something must be done'. Until very recently the assumption was that it would be better if one or both of the old couple went into a home where 'they could be looked after properly'. Now, with a very real possibility in Britain that the elderly's' savings might be exhausted by long-stay residence in a home, this last demand has become distinctly less common. In either case, faced with action which apparently goes beyond self-interest, many feel uneasy and perhaps guilty too. So, to add to the indignities of caring for a senile spouse, the one who cares must cope with pressure from the children as well. Caring for the elderly by the elderly can be a lonely and thoroughly unrewarding business and little to do with self-regarding interest of any kind.

Once again it would appear that the language of autonomy, entitlements and rights-to-be-claimed, is far too one-sided to depict moral action adequately. If it is used exclusively as the only language in this area, it may indeed distort both the way people observe and the way they account for moral behaviour. It effectively reduces morality to self-interest and undermines the very possibility of genuinely moral behaviour. As it so happens, it is also considerably at odds with the accumulated moral wisdom of many religious traditions.

By claiming this, it is not necessary to maintain that the language of autonomy, entitlements and rights is morally wrong: it is simply inadequate. Most people once they have experienced it are deeply committed to personal freedom and are suspicious of doctors or states who wish to decide things

---

⁹ See M. Abrams, D. Gerard and N. Timms (eds), *Values and Social Change in Britain: Studies in the Contemporary Values of Modern Society*, Macmillan, Basingstoke, 1985; and N. Timms, *Family and Citizenship: Values in Contemporary Britain*, Dartmouth, Aldershot, 1992.

needlessly on their behalf and without their consent. Paternalistic doctors and totalitarian states have this much in common – they show little respect for the personal autonomy of others. Ironically they also deny to others a context for effective moral decision-making. As James Mackey argues persuasively in his *Power and Christian Ethics*,[10] to be moral agents people have to be free to make morally wrong decisions: if other people, or even church bodies, deny them this possibility, then they also deny them the possibility of acting as moral agents.

No doubt some individuals really do have to be denied the possibility of doing wrong or, more accurately, of doing further wrong. Every society is forced to contain in prisons pathological rapists and murderers, if only to keep them apart from other people whilst they still feel impelled to rape and murder. At some point in theories of punishment it is difficult to avoid a notion of 'humane containment'. All societies imprison some people simply to contain them whilst it is still highly likely that they will inflict damage on others. Containment is probably an irresistible notion in theories of punishment – even though it is, I believe, a quite disastrous one if it becomes our sole theory of punishment.[11] Nevertheless, for most people the possibility of being able to do what they know to be wrong is a prerequisite of being free to choose what they know to be right. A notion of personal autonomy is essential for an adequate understanding of moral agency.

Again it is not necessary to deny the importance of notions of entitlements and rights. Of course, such notions have proved notoriously difficult to define and even more difficult to reach agreement upon. Rights and counter-rights have been asserted in a number of recent moral debates and have served to confuse many observers of these debates. As noted elsewhere, Alasdair MacIntyre points to the contestation of rights that tends to characterise debates about abortion at the moment;[12] pro-life and pro-choice protagonists soon become locked in charges and counter-charges: both tend to assert inalienable rights which

[10] CUP, Cambridge, 1994.
[11] See further my *Moral Communities*, Exeter University Press, Exeter, 1992.
[12] Alasdair MacIntyre, *After Virtue*, Duckworth, London, 1985 (2nd Ed.).

those on the other side ignore at their peril. Some of these contestations have recently become violent, with people sometimes even prepared to kill each other over issues such as abortion or animal rights. Yet neither side in these contestations has the remotest prospect of convincing the other through moral reasoning.

Nevertheless the United Nations would be considerably impoverished if all notions of rights or entitlements were abolished tomorrow. The notion of human rights has deeply informed attitudes about what is and about what is not acceptable moral behaviour on the part of nations pitted against other nations.[13] Much might be lost if all language about human rights' violations, when applied, for example, to torture and genocide, were to be renounced. Ignorance of the rights of others (acting under military orders) was not accepted as a legitimate defence at Nuremberg. Even media depictions of Bosnia and Serbia typically mix relativist claims about the roles of ideology and religion in political conflicts with un-qualified moral outrage at blatant violations of human rights. A postmodern age has become expert at forgetting the roots of the language of rights which we still use if only as a last resort. *In extremis* we find ourselves driven to such language despite our many intellectual misgivings about it. All of these notions – autonomy, entitlements and rights – have important functions in ethical discourse. Yet what is worrying is the ease with which they are used all too frequently to justify positions based solely upon self-regarding interest. My claim is simply that self-regarding interest, in whatever guise it appears, is inadequate as an exclusive basis of moral behaviour. More than that, on its own it would actually negate the possibility of most forms of moral behaviour. Effective moral behaviour requires us to be concerned about others. Whether we adopt the practical language of responsibility to others, the theoretical language of altruism, or the more Kantian (and indeed Lutheran) language of duty, other-directedness is a require-ment of most forms of moral behaviour. Even forms of utilitarianism require us to be concerned about 'the many' and

[13] cf. Kieran Cronin, *Rights and Christian Ethics*, CUP, Cambridge, 1992.

not simply about ourselves. Fortunately most people seem to recognise this in practice, even if they currently tend to deny it in theory.

This last point about altruism can be illustrated with an example from the medical and social worlds. A generation ago Richard Titmuss' seminal book *The Gift Relationship* argued that altruism could be observed in everyday behaviour.[14] The example that Titmuss took was that of blood donation in Britain. Whereas in some countries blood was sold, not given (with disastrous consequences for haemophiliacs before adequate screening for HIV blood infection), the National Health Service in Britain has relied instead upon volunteers giving blood. There is undoubtedly a benefit to society at large from such a system of blood donation, but there is little obvious benefit to individual donors. They might get a temporary glow from giving blood (although there surely must be more pleasant ways of acquiring such a glow). They even get a badge if they give for long enough (a very small badge it might be added), but little more. Titmuss argued that voluntary blood donation offers a vivid example of everyday altruism. It is giving beyond self-interest.

At the time this was an important reminder that altruism was not just possible (despite philosophical determinists) but also actually existed in everyday life (despite social scientific determinists). Since Titmuss wrote, however, biological determinists have also added a sceptical note about altruism. People are genetically programmed to survive, not to act in an altruistic way, especially if such action interferes with their survival. On this account, apparent acts of altruism are, in fact (like the lioness protecting her young), forms of survival behaviour. The way of the cross, on this account, would appear to be a biological aberration: it is genetic survival alone which is normative. The relatively marginal activity of giving blood does little to counter such biological determinism and may even be related to instincts for human survival. Biology, and particularly genetics, is now the new tool for logical positivists. Once it was philosophy, next it was sociology, but now it is biology which

[14] R. M. Titmuss, *The Gift Relationship*, Allen & Unwin, London, 1970.

has become the final arbiter of knowledge about ourselves (later chapters will return to this theme).

However, once again there may be a an important gap here between theory and actual practice. The current behaviour of those with AIDS, or who are HIV positive, might provide a more significant example of everyday altruistic behaviour than Titmuss' blood donors. AIDS is a serious business and the sexual behaviour of those infected with it touches some of the deepest levels of human feelings. Yet there is evidence suggesting that their behaviour is not simply governed by self-regarding interest. Sufferers are for the most part concerned about others, even to the extent of denying themselves.

Anthony Pinching, a professor of immunology who has treated and counselled hundreds of patients with HIV and AIDS in London, provides crucial evidence about widespread altruism amongst his patients. In general he is concerned to stress that self-interest and public policy usually coincide, which makes his hints about altruism all the more interesting. He argues that it is vital not to consider the treatment of those with HIV and AIDS separately from strategies of prevention. If the spread of the disease is to be prevented, then it is crucial that the co-operation of those already infected is enlisted. The very private, even clandestine, nature of sexual relationships makes outside coercion wholly inappropriate:

> Sexual intercourse results from very basic drives that are not entirely under rational control, ranging from the sexual urge itself through to the wish to bear children. Alcohol and other drugs may further affect the effectiveness of rational control on sexual behaviour.[15]

Given all of this, Pinching argues that sensitive counselling of those who are infected, with the aim of helping them to see that it is in their own interests to modify their behaviour, is a primary requirement of both treatment and prevention.

Self-interest in this context takes several forms. Pinching stresses that it is essential that the physician respects, and is seen to respect, the autonomy of HIV patients – since only in

[15] Anthony J. Pinching, 'AIDS: Health Care Ethics and Society', in R. Gillon (ed), *Principles of Health Care Ethics*, Wiley, Chichester, 1994, p. 905.

this way will they co-operate and thus contribute to prevention:

> This is the nub of the issue: if social or personal disadvantage
> is seen to result from accessing individual care and advice, it
> will either not be sought or the advice not followed. If such
> individual provision is inaccessible or unavailable, public
> education and exhortation may at best be unhelpful, or at
> worst may enhance isolation and demotivate the individual
> from behavioural change. If individuals are not empowered to
> reflect on and to change behaviour in relation to their own
> actual and likely future personal behaviour, the opportunity
> to reduce the frequency of potential transmission events will
> be missed.[16]

Thus, it is in the interests of both individual patients and society
at large for counselling to be accessible and readily available.
Such counselling must respect individual autonomy and, at
most, is attempting to persuade rather than coerce patients. Yet
granted all of this, why should patients who are already infected
modify their sexual behaviour? Pinching points to one self-
interested reason: modifying sexual behaviour reduces the risk
of acquiring other infections that may enhance the progression
of HIV diseases in those who are already HIV positive. But
what if the individual already has full-blown AIDS and what if
his or her desire for unprotected sexual intercourse is greater
than fear of acquiring other infections? It is at this point that
Pinching hints that self-interest is not the whole of the story:

> In my experience, the overwhelming majority of patients with
> HIV infection are all too keen to ensure to protect others
> from the formidable problems they themselves are facing. The
> idea of 'revenge' sex and the like belong more to the realms of
> fiction and tabloid headlines than to reality.[17]

These are important words from a physician of such wide
clinical experience of HIV and AIDS sufferers. Evidently there
are a few individual sufferers who are determinedly self-
interested and who are wholly unprepared to change their
sexual behaviour in order to protect others. As the disease

---

[16] ibid., pp. 907–8.
[17] ibid., p. 909.

spreads societies may well become increasingly alarmed and draconian about them. Many societies already have powers to imprison those who are infected and yet remain promiscuous. Yet that is hardly a solution. Are such people to be imprisoned until they die, if they show no signs of social conformity? And, given the bisexuality of prison life, is prison really a suitable environment for infected males, with the attendant risk of spreading the disease further into the heterosexual population once other prisoners are released? Even the control of prostitution presents formidable logistical difficulties.[18] If enough infected people are determinedly self-interested and cannot be persuaded to consider others, then any society will eventually face huge problems. Yet on Pinching's evidence, at least, mutuality still governs the behaviour of most HIV and AIDS sufferers.

As we gradually face up to some of the massive moral dilemmas confronting our planet at the end of the millennium, so we may slowly begin to realise that mutuality is actually a requirement of human living. Somehow we must persuade people in rich countries to consume less and those in poor countries to have less children – even when it does not seem to be in their personal interests to do so. AIDS is merely one signal that our behaviour as human beings is interdependent.

Most religious traditions have, as already noted, always known this, insisting that true faith requires the faithful to move beyond self-interest. Furthermore, most religious traditions seek to foster worshipping communities that sustain individuals in their attempt to move beyond self-interest. Yet much secular culture imagines that all moral behaviour is in the end based solely upon autonomy and self-interest and that individuals can behave morally without being sustained by communities, let alone by worshipping communities. In contrast, I believe that even in a postmodern age an emphasis upon mutuality and moral communities is essential for church leaders. In the chapters that follow I will seek to explore the moral and theological links that are required here.

---

[18] See further my *Christian Ethics in Secular Worlds*, T&T Clark, Edinburgh, 1991.

## 3

# Moral Communities and Christian Ethics

For the moment the battle seems to have been largely won. Most exponents of Christian ethics today seem to agree that morality has a firm communitarian basis. The understanding of Christian ethics which was often held a generation ago – that it is a discipline concerned primarily with individual moral decision-making – seems to have been routed. The outrageous individualistic paradigms offered by 'situation ethicists' are now a dim memory. Most agree that it is virtue and character within Christian communities that should be the main concern of Christian ethics. There is even a new confidence within Christian ethics. After decades of being patronised by moral philosophy, Christian ethicists have become distinctly more apologetic and polemical. Christian ethicists also express increasing scepticism about the ability of moral philosophers to be able to resolve dilemmas with universally convincing rational arguments. In short, the key contentions of *After Virtue* have triumphed.

There is even a symmetry between this triumph and the popular view of the churches. Despite the fact that only one in ten people in Britain are in church on a typical Sunday and that two-thirds of the population seldom if ever goes to church at all, there still seems to be a widespread popular belief that 'religion' and perhaps even religious institutions are important for the maintenance of morality. Moral behaviour in society is thought to be dependent upon an over-spill from 'religion'. It is not too important what a person's religious beliefs actually are, provided she does have some. That alone is sufficient to ensure decent, moral behaviour. Whilst few theologians would express this link between morality and faith so crudely, they increasingly argue that moral virtue is a product of moral communities and that a transcendent faith offers a more secure foundation for such communities than does secularism. It is precisely these links – between morality and faith, between morality and communities, and between communities and faith – that have encouraged the new boldness in Christian ethics. So, when MacIntyre teases his fellow moral philosophers about their interminable and unresolvable moral conflicts unless they too make such links, naturally many Christian ethicists are delighted. Now it is our turn to taunt secular, atomistic, individualistic liberalism. Without faith and without faith communities such liberalism is morally bankrupt. Once deconstructed this liberalism turns out to be a creed – an undeclared faith – masquerading as common sense or even as empiricism and it is a creed which is unable to justify or resolve its own moral claims.

Perhaps it is not too surprising that the current status of Christian ethics is actually more complicated than all of this might suggest, although a fuller account will have to wait for a later study. Whilst I am convinced by the general thrust of post-MacIntyre Christian ethics, I also believe that it often underestimates some of the theological and sociological problems involved. It tends to produce a theological understanding of churches as moral communities which underestimates the synchronic and diachronic plurality of Christian resources. In addition it tends to produce a picture of churches as moral communities which fits ill their social reality. It can also treat the 'secular' world as being more secular than it actually is: a postmodern age is distinctly more complex than a secular age. The challenge I believe is to find ways of expressing Christian distinctiveness which do not exaggerate the theological and sociological distinctiveness of churches as moral communities. As yet this is a challenge which has occupied the attention of too few Christian ethicists. Making grand claims is just too easy. Making claims which actually fit the ambiguities of churches and society is much more difficult.

There are three levels at which the links between Christian ethics and moral communities can be explored. In sociological language these are the levels of legitimation, socialisation and institutionalisation. In more theological terms they concern the issues of justification and apologetics, Christian nurture and formation, and ecclesiology. Each of these levels raises the issue of plurality as a dominant problem and each requires a different range of methodological skills. An adequate understanding of Christian ethics and moral communities requires an inter-disciplinary approach. A fundamental weakness of the literature that takes this approach to Christian ethics seriously is that it gives inadequate attention to each of these three levels. This can be illustrated by looking briefly at George Lindbeck's understanding of theology and morality. It has been a powerful influence on Stanley Hauerwas and others within Christian ethics.

Lindbeck's *The Nature of Doctrine* has rapidly become a seminal text.[1] What he offers is a very remarkable cultural-linguistic understanding of the nature of doctrine which he believes is particularly suitable for a post-liberal age. *The Nature of Doctrine* is simultaneously a theological critique of secularism, a theological response to Wittgenstein and a radical statement of the distinctiveness of Christian (and indeed religious) faith and morality. All of this is a considerable achievement for so short a book.

Lindbeck distinguishes three 'ideal types' of theological approach. The first he depicts as the cognitive-propositional approach which sees doctrines as informative propositions to be assessed cognitively. Following the logic of this approach Christian ethics is the discipline that derives moral positions from doctrinal propositions. It is the business of the systematic theologian to establish a normative set of orthodox beliefs and it is the business of the moral theologian to work out the ethical consequences of these beliefs once established. The second he depicts as experiential-expressive which, in contrast, sees doctrines as less to do with cognition and more to do with feelings and inner experience. On this approach theology often

[1] See further my *Readings in Modern Theology*, SPCK, London, and Abingdon, New York, 1995.

takes on a directly moral function. Within some liberal and
existentialist constructions doctrines and moral prescriptions
are virtually identical. The third ideal type Lindbeck depicts as
cultural-linguistic. According to this theology, and indeed
religion in general, is more like a language and a culture. It
belongs essentially to communities which generate their own
rules of discourse and morality. If the first type is characteristic
of classical theology and the second of liberal theology, then the
third is the type that Lindbeck believes is most appropriate for a
post-liberal society in which the assumptions of a common
secular rationality no longer prevail.

Each of these types represents a distinct way of doing
theology 'embedded in a conceptual framework so comprehensive that it shapes its own criteria of adequacy':

> What propositionalists with their stress on unchanging truth
> and falsity regard as faithful, applicable, and intelligible is likely
> to be dismissed as dead orthodoxy by liberal experiential-
> expressivists. Conversely, the liberal claim that change and
> pluralism in religious expression are necessary for intelligibility,
> applicability, and faithfulness is attacked by the propositionally
> orthodox as an irrationally relativistic and practically self-
> defeating betrayal of the faith. A postliberal might propose to
> overcome this polarization between tradition and innovation
> by a distinction between the abiding doctrinal grammar and
> variable theological vocabulary, but this proposal appears from
> other perspectives as the worst of two worlds rather than the
> best of both.[2]

This helpful distinction does indeed clarify some of the mutual
misunderstandings that often characterise theology in general
and Christian ethics in particular. Seen as 'ideal types' these
three approaches to theology clearly generate very different
agendas and they do help us to understand better some of
the considerable pluralism evident within theology. Those
adopting a predominantly propositional approach are likely
to be unimpressed by those adopting a predominantly experi-
ential approach. And neither of them may make much sense of

---

[2] George A. Lindbeck, *The Nature of Doctrine: Religion and Theology in a Postliberal
Age*, Westminster Press, Philadelphia, and SPCK, London, 1984, p. 113.

those who adopt a predominately cultural-linguistic approach.

That said, I am not sure that Lindbeck really adheres to his own depiction of these approaches as 'ideal types'. For Weber it was essential to remind his readers that 'ideal types' are simply heuristic devices. They are not to be confused with social reality itself which is always more messy. Social reality, like biological reality, does not come packaged into watertight types with strictly delineated boundaries. Hence my use of the word 'predominantly' in relation to these three theological approaches. Even the most propositionally oriented theologian does tend at times to make connections with living experience and few experiential-expressivist theologians adopt the Cupitt path of thoroughgoing non-realism (a path which, in any case, always has difficulty with the status of its own claims – since if they too are non-realist then presumably we can take them or leave them according to our particular preference).

Although he defends a cultural-linguistic approach to theology in a suitably modest way, it is clear that Lindbeck believes that it does offer an ecumenical way through current theological pluralism which at the same time takes the challenge of Wittgenstein seriously. For Christianity it is the canonical scriptures which constitute its distinctive cultural-linguistic resource:

> For those who are steeped in them, no world is more real than the ones they create. A scriptural world is thus able to absorb the universe. It supplies the interpretive framework within which believers seek to live their lives and understand reality. This happens quite apart from formal theories. Augustine did not describe his work in the categories we are employing, but the whole of his theological production can be understood as a progressive, even if not always successful, struggle to insert everything from Platonism and the Pelagian problem to the fall of Rome into the world of the Bible. Aquinas tried to do something similar with Aristotelianism, and Schleiermacher with German romantic idealism. The way they described extrascriptural realities and experience, so it can be argued, was shaped by biblical categories much more than was warranted by their formal methodologies.[3]

[3] ibid., p. 117.

There are some very telling elements in this quotation. Lindbeck is determined to insist that it is the canonical scriptures which constitute the cultural-linguistic resource of theology. Yet he honestly admits that some of the classical (and, of course, modern) theologians did not seem to appreciate this for themselves. His argument might just work for the profoundly scriptural Augustine, but it looks distinctly thinner in relation to Aquinas and Schleiermacher. What Lindbeck seems to be saying is that theologians such as Aquinas (who certainly used the Bible extensively but whose arguments often rested upon non-biblical authorities) and Schleiermacher were more scripturally oriented than they realised themselves. It is at this point that Lindbeck's theory ceases to be a descriptive account of theology based upon 'ideal types'. It now appears as a prescriptive theory based rather upon real types. Indeed, shortly after this quotation he claims that 'there is always a danger . . . that the extrabiblical materials inserted into the biblical universe will themselves become the basic framework of interpretation'.[4]

There is an oscillation between description and prescription and between ideal and actual types in Lindbeck's *The Nature of Doctrine* which makes it hard to pin down. Viewed as a prescriptive actual-type book, it seems to offer a clear but contentious path for Christian ethics. What it appears to suggest is that in a post-liberal age, when common culture and secular rationality have completely broken down, religious communities still have their own distinctive cultural-linguistic resources. In the major religions these are all derived from an authoritative scripture of one sort or another. For Christians the canonical resources of the Old and New Testaments (the Apocrypha is more problematic) constitute their distinctive scriptural resource. Christian ethics, in turn, derives entirely from this cultural-linguistic resource. It is the product of communities that have been shaped by canonical Scripture. Christian ethics is thus communitarian, scriptural and distinctive.

Although this offers a clear path for Christian ethics, it does so only by cutting corners in terms of my three levels of

---

[4] ibid., p. 118.

legitimation, socialisation and institutionalisation. I think that Lindbeck himself is aware of this and I doubt if he is finally offering such a clear-cut understanding of Christian ethics. At most he is probably offering an emphasis. Nevertheless there is some value in setting out some of the problems that would confront a clear-cut understanding of his theory.

First legitimation. Lindbeck's subtitle – *Religion and Theology in a Postliberal Age* – already suggests that something is wrong, or at least exaggerated. There is, of course, the huge claim to be talking about 'religion' as well as about theology. It soon becomes evident that he basically has in mind those 'religions' which have scriptures, since they alone conform to his cultural-linguistic theory of religion. He does refer in passing to Evans-Pritchard's account of religion amongst the Nuer, but only because he wishes to show how fragile this form of religion is when confronted with scriptural religion. With breathtaking cheek he argues that it 'helps explain why purely customary religions and cultures readily dissolve under the pressure of historical, social and linguistic change . . . it also suggests that canonical texts are a condition, not only for the survival of a religion but for the very possibility of normative theological description.'[5] David Ford points out that this account of 'religion' seems to be thoroughly biased in favour of Christianity. Yet having made that criticism he immediately points out that 'this need only be confirmation of Lindbeck's denial of any neutral framework: just as motives for interreligious dialogue may vary, so the ways of conceiving the various religions may be found to be irreducibly related to the categories of one'.[6]

Exactly. Herein lies the major problem for the most clear-cut version of Lindbeck's thesis. According to it we live in an unambiguously postliberal or postmodern age (in this context the two terms are probably indistinguishable). There are no longer any shared bases of knowledge in this age. The rationalist assumptions of modernity have broken down and now we can *only* speak truth 'as we see it' and from the perspectives of the

[5] ibid., p. 116.
[6] David Ford's review of *The Nature of Doctrine* in *Journal of Theological Studies*, Vol. 37, 1986, p. 281.

communities to which we belong. On this understanding there are no neutral planks: foundationalism has been abandoned. We exist only in local cultural-linguistic communities. From within these communities we can discover values and truth, but these are not values and truth which are accessible to others outside these communities. In a postmodern age we live in closed hermeneutical circles.

In the chapter that follows I will place this response to postmodernity into a broader context. For the moment it is worth observing that if we really do live in such closed hermeneutical circles, then rational discourse – presupposed in our very ability to understand Lindbeck's argument – would seem to collapse. David Tracy, Lindbeck's most prestigious rival in the United States, has repeatedly argued that we actually live in a society which is a confusing mixture of modernity and postmodernity.[7] The confident secular individualism of the logical positivists is indeed in a state of considerable disrepair. Yet even that has yet to disappear, as Richard Dawkins demonstrates. Lindbeck even reminds himself at times that 'the present psychosocial situation is more favourable to liberalism than to postliberalism. Sociologists have been telling us for a hundred years or more that the rationalization, pluralism, and mobility of modern life dissolve the bonds of tradition and community.'[8] Yet, having made this concession, there is little in his cultural-linguistic theory which seems to recall it.

One way to depict the complexity of culture today is to see it as a confusing mixture of postmodernity and globalisation. I will return to this in more detail in the final chapter in this book. Briefly, if postmodernity tends to fragment knowledge, morality and truth, driving some of us back to local communities, globalisation tends to reinforce atomistic individualism underpinned by a rationalistic, instrumental and functionalist view of the world. The pressures towards globalisation[9] – reinforced by international travel, trade, entertainment and

---

[7] e.g. David Tracy 'Theology and the Many Faces of Postmodernity', *Theology Today*, Vol. 51, No. 1, April 1994, pp. 104–14.

[8] Lindbeck, op. cit., p. 126.

[9] cf. Roland Robertson, *Globalization: Social Theory and Global Culture*, Sage, London, 1992, and Peter Beyer, *Religion and Globalization*, Sage, London, 1994.

communication – tend to relativise local communities and marginalise local forms of morality. For instance, globalisation makes it difficult for young people throughout the world to resist promiscuous sex, drugs and urban crime, and, in epidemiological terms, it also helps to spread AIDS. The ineluctable nature of globalisation makes it a force that in practice changes individuals and even whole communities – however antagonistic they are to it in theory. In theory we might wish to opt out of consumerism – deploring First World waste and despairing of Third World over-population: in practice most Westerners are deeply committed to consumerism – even arguing at times that increasing consumerism is the solution to Third World over-population. We are all trapped by globalisation, even whilst we feel the counter forces of postmodernity. And the most extreme products of both of these forces are fellow citizens in many parts of the world today. Thus, postmodern fundamentalists live side by side in America, the Middle East and elsewhere with secularised individualists. It is precisely their juxtaposition that has proved so inflammatory in the late twentieth century – as Salman Rushdie uncomfortably discovered in 'modern' Britain.

It is in the context of this deep cultural ambiguity that local communities become more important at the level of socialisation rather than legitimation. Lindbeck is surprisingly unhelpful about this second level of analysis. His cultural-linguistic theory clearly presupposes that Christian communities are shaped through Scripture. He is well aware that approaches to Scripture have varied very considerably both synchronically and diachronically. He has also become increasingly bleak about the ability of churches in present-day America [or Britain] to mediate Scripture successfully.[10] Anyone teaching theology in secular universities in Britain or in America will be only too aware that the scriptural knowledge of the average student is extremely limited. Even those who still come from conventional Christian backgrounds may have a very sketchy acquaintance with the Bible. Not only were

[10] See his article in R. N. Bellah (ed), *Postmodern Theology: Christian Faith in a Pluralist World*, Harper, San Francisco, 1989.

previous generations more familiar with the Bible, but they even had a single version, the Authorised Version, from which they could quote in common. Today, in contrast, biblical allusions within classical English literature are simply lost on most students.

Whilst many might lament the cultural poverty resulting from this change, for Lindbeck it is a catastrophic theological loss. The cultural-linguistic resource, on which Christianity, Christian doctrine and Christian ethics depend, is increasingly lost for the present generation. The theological and moral truths which derive directly from a culture soaked in Scripture are no longer accessible to those who are unschooled in the Bible. The scriptural community which lies at the heart of Christian religion is fast being eroded.

I would not wish to underestimate the cultural and religious loss that results from this general decline in biblical knowledge. However I do not believe it is the only major religious loss in our society. There have, after all, been forms of Christian community, especially before the ages of the printed word, which have known very little about the contents of the Bible. Presumably on Lindbeck's theory they must almost be disallowed as being Christian. In this respect Dennis Nineham remains an extremely uncomfortable scholar, arguing that there is not too much in common between Christian communities viewed diachronically.[11] Even synchronically there may be very major problems. The Catholic sociologist Joseph Fitzpatrick discovers quite startling differences within present-day American Catholicism. The Catholicism of the Kennedys has precious little in common with the Catholicism of Hispanic illegal immigrants.[12] To depict all of these as communities shaped basically by canonical scripture appears more than slightly optimistic.

A better case might be made for regarding worship rather than canonical scripture as the most distinctive feature of

---

[11] Dennis Nineham, *Christianity Mediaeval and Modern*, SCM Press, London, 1993.

[12] Joseph Fitzpatrick, *One Church Many Cultures: The Challenge of Diversity*, Sheed & Ward, New York, 1987. See also Michael Hornsby-Smith, *Roman Catholicism in England*, CUP, Cambridge, *1987*, and *Roman Catholic Beliefs in England*, CUP, Cambridge, 1991.

Christianity in an ambiguously secular world. Worship is also a feature of other religions too and there are many aspects of worship that Jews, Christians and Muslims have in common – but that is not my concern here. Specifically within Christianity, worship is a feature that characterises all churches in all ages. Sometimes it has taken the form of written, corporate liturgies, but sometimes not. Sometimes it has been exclusively biblical in content (most fully in the Sandemanian sect), but sometimes it has made little direct use of the Bible. Sometimes public worship has involved full congregational participation, but sometimes it has been dominated by religious professionals. Considerable variety and indeed plurality is evident in worship, but it is nonetheless particularly distinctive in a society in which two-thirds of the population never takes part in public worship and many of them no longer even pray in private. It can even be argued that it is worship which gives substance to religious language and which is a key feature in doctrinal formulation – *lex orandi: lex credendi.*[13]

There do also seem to be important empirical links between worship and both moral attitudes and moral behaviour. A number of surveys[14] have now shown that regular church-going is correlated with stances on moral issues (usually rather conservative stances). However, returning to the theme of altruism, the European Value Systems surveys have in-structively suggested that regular churchgoing is strongly correlated with unpaid voluntary work in the community. For example, the 1990 survey found that 27% of voluntary workers claimed to go to church at least once a week – a figure almost three times above the national churchgoing rate. And in the 1981 survey attendance at religious services at least once a month was found to be the most significant variable – for once ahead of gender, age or social class – predicting whether someone is involved in voluntary work.

[13] cf. Geoffrey Wainwright, *Doxology: The Praise of God in Worship, Doctrine and Life: A Systematic Theology*, Epworth Press, London, 1980.

[14] For full details of these see my *Moral Communities*, Exeter University Press, Exeter, 1992, pp. 16–20. For the European Value Systems surveys see M. Abrams, D. Gerard and N. Timms (eds), *Values and Social Change in Britain: Studies in the Contemporary Values of Modern Society*, Macmillan, Basingstoke, 1985, and N. Timms, *Family and Citizenship: Values in Contemporary Britain*, Dartmouth, Aldershot, 1992.

But what is it about worship that affects moral attitudes and behaviour? Is it the cognitive contents of worship – of which one important element is usually (but not always) Scripture? Or is it less cognitive features such as 'belonging' and the mutual encouragement to look beyond ourselves that collective worship offers? The findings of the Princeton sociologist Robert Wuthnow on support groups in modern America are particularly helpful. As he points out, it has for long been an aphorism that America is a society of determined individualists – ranging from the rugged individualism of the pioneers through to the atomism of today leading to a steady erosion of families and local communities. Yet this vision of American society has tended to ignore the recent proliferation of support groups – church groups, self-help groups, therapy groups and so forth. On the basis of his extensive research Wuthnow estimates that 40% of the American population now belongs to such groups. Community in the sense of face-to-face support groups is far from dead in this apparently most individualistic of societies.

Wuthnow's investigations of members of these support groups provide some crucial data about religious socialisation and about the specific links between communities and moral attitudes and behaviour. The popular perception of such groups is that they are inward looking and concerned only with individual self-improvement. Surprisingly, Wuthnow finds that they are actually rather successful in encouraging altruistic behaviour and attitudes. Whilst 77% of those surveyed did work 'with the group to help someone inside the group', 62% also worked 'with the group to help other people in need outside of the group'. 56% reported that as a result of belonging to the group they had become more interested in peace or social justice and 43% had become involved in work in the community. 57% of those in the groups also donated to other charitable organisations. Specifically church-based group members reported that as a result of their membership they now took a more active part in other programmes sponsored by their church (62%) and had increased their giving to their church (50%). Wuthnow finds that belonging to a small group in a church is in fact more important than any other religious indicator:

Small group participation . . . makes more of a difference than any other measure of religious commitment. To be precise, participation distinguishes between volunteers and non-volunteers better than any of the following: how important religion was to people as they were growing up, how often they attended religious services while growing up, how important religion is to them now, whether they believe Jesus is God, whether they feel they have committed their lives to Jesus, whether they are a church member, how often they attend religious services, whether they pray, and whether they have had a deep religious experience. For example, when predicting whether people will do volunteer work for social service and welfare organizations, being in a small fellowship group predicts about twice as strongly as any of these other factors.[15]

From all of this Wuthnow concludes that, 'despite the fact that most small groups . . . focus on the emotional needs and interests of their members, they nevertheless nudge the people to become involved in helping friends and neighbors who are not members of their group and to play an active role in voluntary agencies'.[16] Such groups encourage members to become more active both in their churches and in their local communities. For Wuthnow it is the mutual support, encouragement and sense of belonging that are crucial in these groups – rather than their specifically cognitive contents.

This finding seems to fit well the sort of research being undertaken recently by Wayne Meeks in his *The Origins of Christian Morality*. Like Lindbeck (whom he does not cite) Meeks too, is interested in Christian culture. Unlike Lindbeck he does not discover in the New Testament a single distinctive Christian culture. Rather he finds a series of Christian cultures which overlap considerably with other first- and second-century cultures. He acknowledges a strong debt to MacIntyre's *After Virtue* and takes from it the notion that morality is not embedded or supported in culture primarily through rational means. Instead the means of socialisation through which

[15] Robert Wuthnow, *Sharing the Journey: Support Groups and America's New Quest for Community*, The Free Press, New York, 1994, p. 328.
[16] ibid., p. 330.

morality becomes established are various and complex. It is
Meeks' aim to uncover some of these means as they appear in
and beyond the New Testament:

> If I am right about the way moral dispositions are shaped and
> the way they work in a community, then a description of early
> Christian morality cannot be limited to an account of the
> 'Christian' theological ideas that bear on ethics, or of their
> moral rules, or of the structures of their moral arguments –
> though these all have a place in the description. Rather we
> approach them as if we were ethnographers of the past,
> inquiring about the forms of culture within which the ethical
> sensibilities of the early Christians have meaning.[17]

Accordingly Meeks sets out to analyse texts from a variety of
perspectives – sometimes as the words of communities of new
converts, sometimes in terms of communities alternately loving
and hating the world, sometimes as lists of vices (or virtues),
sometimes in terms of the language of obligation, sometimes in
terms of heroic examples, sometimes in terms of a cruciform
structure of suffering. What he discloses in the process is a series
of moral communities constituting together what we now term
'early Christianity'. It is a picture considerably more complex
and varied than the communities shaped by canonical scripture
which are fundamental to Lindbeck's theory. Perhaps the
pluriform worlds of local belonging discovered by Wuthnow
and Meeks are not so far apart. Christian socialisation is
and may always have been local, communal and varied –
having little in common other than Christocentric worship and
through that a moral concern beyond self-interest.

There is a final level at which all of this can be examined –
that of institutionalisation But here I will be briefer as this level
has occupied my writings so much in the past. If the primary
means of socialisation in Christian morality is the worshipping
congregation or, even more intensively, the church group, what
implications does this have for church bodies which feel
impelled to pronounce on moral issues? Already the ambiguous
social context within which Western Christianity is set and the

---

[17] Wayne A. Meeks, *The Origins of Christian Morality: The First Two Centuries*, Yale
University Press, New Haven and London, 1993, p. 11.

varied and complex networks of local groups, congregations and communities that make up earliest and present-day Christianity should offer a clear warning. It is extremely unlikely that churches as a whole will be able plausibly to offer single moral perspectives. If plurality is characteristic of the levels of both legitimation and socialisation, then plurality might be expected at the institutional level too. Ian Markham has argued instructively in his *Plurality and Christian Ethics*[18] that British churches, unlike their American counterparts, have been rather too reluctant to come to terms with their evident plurality.

However there is an obvious way of eliminating this plurality, which James Mackey analyses starkly in his *Power and Christian Ethics*. It is quite simply coercion. Faced with evident Christian plurality, any church that wishes to present an undivided moral or doctrinal message to the world can do so if it resorts to coercion. Mackey locates power on a spectrum between force and moral authority. The exercise of power which he sees as typical of Jesus as presented in the Gospels is power as moral authority. However the exercise of power which as a Catholic he sees as endemic within his own church (and for good measure within many Reformed churches too) is power as force. So, faced with a policy on contraception that 'has outlasted any convincing memory of the cultural circumstances in which it was first borrowed or created',[19] he believes that his church can only resort to coercion to uphold its 'unified' claims on the subject. Papal authority, he argues, is accordingly bolstered through coercive means – such as the suppression of dissident voices amongst Catholic moral theologians and the appointment of an increasingly conservative episcopacy. Yet in the process it loses any claim to moral authority.

Elsewhere I have outlined four alternative paths[20] which recognise Christian plurality more plausibly: the individual prophet, the uniform sect, the inter-church movement, and the values-in-tension of the church. The first three can proclaim unified moral positions, but they may not expect to represent the whole of Christianity or the whole of Christian opinion.

[18] CUP, Cambridge, 1994.
[19] James P. Mackey, *Power and Christian Ethics*, CUP, Cambridge, 1994, p. 210.
[20] See chapter 4 of *Moral Communities*.

The individual prophet and the uniform sect can be deeply at odds with, and even radically opposed to, both society at large and the churches. The prophet characteristically believes that her legitimation and message come directly from God. Such a prophet offers a degree of moral purity not available to other Christians – a moral purity that may be deeply disturbing and, in time, might even be considered to be profoundly mistaken. Both the prophet and the exclusivist sect (I am aware of huge variations in sect typologies) can proclaim and denounce and tend to stand apart from society and from more conventional Christians. The inter-church movement, in contrast, typically is formed by mainline Christians who are at odds with their denominations on a single issue – be it the ordination of women or the possession of nuclear weapons – and who wish to lobby for change or perhaps just gather for comfort and mutual support. The single issue is the *raison d'être* of the inter-church movement.

Churches, on the other hand, are notoriously (and perhaps inevitably) divided on most moral issues. Philip Wogaman concludes his study of the history of Christian ethics as follows:

> Christians have arrived at opposite conclusions about many things, such as war, slavery, the role of women, wealth, sexual relationships, politics, and even the more commonplace virtues. That fact alone would be scandalous if one thought of the tradition as a deposit of truth 'once for all delivered to the saints'. But if one thinks rather of the tradition as a witness to the transcendent reality of the living God, then is there not room for growth and new insight?[21]

What Wogaman expresses here is a classic church type response to Christian ethics – recognising frankly the evident divisions that exist amongst Christians, but looking to some unity in diversity beyond them. On this approach (which I finally share myself) the most we can expect to have in common are biblically consonant values or virtues held in tension – tension between peace and justice, between rights and duties, between grace and law, between the mundane and the sacred, and so

---

[21] J. Philip Wogaman, *Christian Ethics: A Historical Introduction*, Westminster/John Knox Press, Louisville, and SPCK, London, 1993, p. 270.

forth. Yet, like Wogaman, I believe that such a perspective can indeed lead to maturity and growth.

I am more than conscious that each of these three levels of analysis – legitimation, socialisation and institutionalisation – require separate and lengthy treatment. I hope soon to be able to give them that.[22] All that should be clear by now is that I do not find the clear-cut interpretation of Lindbeck's theory adequate for Christian ethics. Despite its influence upon Stanley Hauerwas and others, it seems to me that it considerably underestimates plurality both within Christian ethics and within the complex world that the discipline seeks to serve. Tempting as it might be for moral leaders in a postmodern age, it should be treated with circumspection.

[22] For my series *New Studies in Christian Ethics*, CUP.

# 4

## Reinhold Niebuhr and Postmodernity

In a postmodern or pluralistic age how is Christian distinctiveness to be identified? In one form or another this question
recurs throughout the chapters in this book. A number of
younger theologians have returned to the writings of Karl
Barth for an answer. Robin Lovin's study of Reinhold Niebuhr[1]
offers a fascinating alternative for those of us who find Barth
problematic. Of course, neither Barth nor Niebuhr knew of
the recent debate about postmodernity, yet they were clearly
aware of twentieth-century pluralism and fragmentation and
of the fragility of the Christian witness in such a context. It is
not too difficult to set them into a broad map of possible
Christian responses to postmodernity. Three are particularly
relevant:

The first is the most radical and Barthian. It argues that
legitimation is only possible within cultural-linguistic communities and that such communities are incapable of mutual
communication. Precisely because the independent 'planks'
offered by modernism (notably autonomous rational thought
and empirical demonstration) have now been deconstructed,
moral values or virtues can only be known within specific
communities. It has already been seen that Lindbeck provides
an example of this approach. By extension Christian ethicists
such as Stanley Hauerwas and John Milbank also seem to be
exponents of it.

[1] Robin W. Lovin, *Reinhold Niebuhr and Christian Realism*, CUP, Cambridge and
New York, 1995.

The second maintains that communities can communicate with each other precisely because individuals in the West today typically each belong to more than one community. In his writings since *After Virtue* MacIntyre has sought to trace ways in which communities overlap and in which legitimation may sometimes decline in one at the expense of another. Jonathan Sacks, to whom I shall return in the next section, is an able theological exponent of the moral implications of simultaneously belonging to two communities – in his case those of a pluralist society and a traditional Jewish community.

However, if the claims of globalisation are also taken seriously – as I shall argue in the final chapter in this book – then a third response to postmodernism is also possible. Whilst accepting the general position that moral values and virtues are shaped, sustained and carried in communities, this third position argues that there *are* some moral 'planks' that apply across cultures. A number of postmodern Catholic theologians have suggested such a modified 'natural law' approach, including Lisa Sowle Cahill's *Sex, Gender and Christian Ethics*[2] and Jean Porter's *Moral Action and Christian Ethics.*[3]

It is possible that MacIntyre may also be moving in the direction of this third approach. In responding to a variety of critics in a recent collection, rather predictably called *After MacIntyre*, he does seem to suggest this. One of the most distinguished critics/admirers in the collection is Charles Taylor. In a somewhat diffuse essay on 'Justice after Virtue' he agrees with MacIntyre that the demands of historic communities are important, but in contrast to MacIntyre he still maintains that 'disengaged' individual rational agency remains significant. In effect he wishes to accept both post-modernist and modernist claims. For Taylor:

> [MacIntyre] tends to take modern society at the face value of its own dominant theories, as heading for runaway atomism and break-up. He speaks at times of a society organized around 'emotivist' understandings of ethics. I, on the other hand,

[2] Lisa Sowle Cahill, *Sex, Gender and Christian Ethics*, CUP, Cambridge and New York, 1996.

[3] Jean Porter, *Moral Action and Christian Ethics*, CUP, Cambridge and New York, 1995.

frankly lean in the other direction. I think that we are far more 'Aristotelian' than we allow, that hence our practice is in some significant way less based on pure disengaged freedom and atomism than we realize.[4]

However, MacIntyre argues that such a both/and solution introduces incoherence and makes moral judgments about justice finally more difficult to achieve. He is convinced that moral practice within historic communities already contains sufficient standards for identifying and condemning moral deformations and distortions, without any recourse to disengaged 'objective' rationality.

Expressed rather differently, MacIntyre's Thomist critics share Taylor's concern about the need for some 'objective' standards. For example, Janet Coleman in her essay on 'MacIntyre and Aquinas' argues that the Thomist understanding of natural law is rather different from MacIntyre's notion of historically embedded practice:

> For Aristotle and Aquinas there may indeed be a history of practices, a history of the means to ends, but the defining standards by which they may be judged have no history, they are universals absolutely, they are the natures or essences grasped by the definition of their goal. Hence MacIntyre, in asserting that standards are not immune from criticism, misunderstands how Aristotle and Aquinas define practices in terms of what they aim to achieve, their ends.[5]

John Haldane, too, expresses doubts about how far MacIntyre's position is consistent with that of Aquinas in facing such issues as historical relativism.

MacIntyre, in response, does concede some ground to these two critics. However he also believes that they are, at least in part, responding to very different questions. His notion of historical embeddedness largely concerns both the apprenticeship to any tradition-constituted practice and the boundaries across traditions, whereas Coleman is more concerned with 'the

---

[4] John Horton and Susan Mendus (eds), *After MacIntyre: Critical Perspectives on the Work of Alasdair MacIntyre*, Polity Press, Oxford, and University of Notre Dame Press, Notre Dame, Indiana, 1994, p. 22.

[5] ibid., p. 91.

nature of rational justification and of that attainment of truth which constitutes the telos of rational enquiry'.[6] Viewed as different dimensions, he maintains that his position and that of Coleman and Aquinas are not incompatible.

It is precisely at this point that Robin Lovin's excellent study of Reinhold Niebuhr becomes relevant. Lovin seeks to trace three inter-related dimensions of Christian realism in Niebuhr's writings: theistic, moral and political. In the opening chapters he explores this relationship in the sequence of the political followed by the moral and then the theistic. In some ways this is the easiest way to grasp the interrelationship. However in the chapters that follow he starts with the theistic, then has two chapters on the moral, whilst a fourth chapter is given to the political. The whole sequence is then finally related to the issue of justice in Niebuhr's writings.

Lovin shows that these dimensions are indeed related to each other in Niebuhr's writings. There is a facile secular use of Niebuhr which reduces his thought to a form of political pragmatism and ignores the fact that behind his ideas there is always a theistic vision of a God of love transcending political processes. Precisely because Niebuhr became famous (or notorious) for his scorn of what he regarded as facile utopianism, for his dismissal of pacifism and non-violent Christian action in a context of overwhelming totalitarian power, and for his apparent separation of individual moral behaviour from amoral corporate behaviour, it is sometime forgotten that his theology did contain a strong eschatological notion of divine love. Lovin successfully shows that this notion was indeed central to Niebuhr's concept of political realism. Niebuhr's notion of the reality of God also ensured that he was a moral realist – despite his characteristic (but not always consistent) antagonism to natural law theory. Anyone who has read the tortuous passages on *justitia originalis* in his Gifford Lectures will be aware of this characteristic, but perhaps somewhat confused, element in Niebuhr's thought.

What Lovin attempts to show is that Christian realism – albeit shorn of some of Niebuhr's defects – still offers a dis-

---

[6] ibid., p. 300.

tinctively Christian path in Christian ethics. Christian realism is not simply liberalism sanctifying the secular with a detachable theological overlay: nor is it a form of neo-orthodoxy removing theology virtually or actually from empirical reality. To use modern jargon, Christian realism is contextualised theology which remains distinctively Christian in thought and orientation. Lovin defines this approach as follows:

> The dynamics of history are driven by the human capacity always to imagine life beyond existing limitations. Biblical faith gives vision and direction to that capacity for self-transcendence, but we are best able to challenge and channel our powers when we also understand what is really going on.[7]

Despite his obvious approval of Niebuhr's overall vision of Christian realism, Lovin finds himself forced to be rather clearer than Reinhold (but not Richard) Niebuhr was himself:

> Niebuhr gives little time to definition in his work. His aims are synthetic, linking related ideas into a complex whole, rather than strictly delimiting the individual elements. His method is dialectical, in the sense that concepts are clarified by stating what they exclude, and positions are explained by specifying what they reject . . . Niebuhr's position emerges as a complex of theological conviction, moral theory, and meditation on human nature in which the elements are mutually reinforcing rather than systematically related . . . We understand what Christian Realism is largely by identifying the many less adequate views that it is not.[8]

The convoluted style of Niebuhr, allied to a chronic reluctance to define his terms, was what seemed so to annoy people like William Temple (as well no doubt as a touch of English snobbery!). Lovin's three dimensions of Christian realism are a very helpful way of unravelling Niebuhr from his own convolutions and, indeed, of finding a route through the contortions of postmodernity today.

[7] Lovin, op. cit., p. 1.
[8] ibid., p. 3.

## *Dimension 1: God*

Lovin argues that in his day Niebuhr's notion of 'theological realism' challenged both liberalism and neo-orthodoxy. Faced with the pointed question that Jeffrey Stout[9] poses today to theologians – namely, what new claims about the human situation do we make by saying that God is present in the needs or goals that are common to humanity? – Niebuhr rejected both the practical atheism so often encountered in liberalism and the denial of any common human needs and goals frequently encountered in neo-orthodoxy. For him theology was neither an optional overlay nor a complete alternative to secular analysis. Theology is neither reducible to psychology, political analysis, sociology, or whatever, nor is it an alternative to such disciplines:

> The complex interactions of interest groups, historical forces, and persistent human needs for power and security each demand their own elaborate theoretical explanations, and Niebuhr can be eloquent in his analysis of the social strains imposed by class conflicts or the ideological justifications that palliate inequalities of wealth and privilege. In the end, however, human conflict and human aspirations must be understood in relation to God, who sets limits on the conflict and affirms human unity, while at the same time judging every particular attempt to formulate that unity and every claim to have achieved it.[10]

Thus, through political analysis (or whatever) alone there is no final possibility of unity. It is only through faith in God that we can find a 'final unity which transcends the world's chaos'. Theological beliefs should cohere with our other beliefs but they do not have to succumb to all beliefs and especially not to relativism: 'Realistic theology . . . rejects the interpretations that leap from the diversity of beliefs to a theory of relativism, but it must be equally critical of the moral certainty to which religious communities are susceptible. When a religious institution claims "unconditional truth for its doctrines and

---

[9] Jeffrey Stout, *Ethics After Babel: The Language of Morals and Their Discontents*, James Clarke, New York, 1988.
[10] Lovin, op. cit., pp. 35–6.

unconditioned moral authority for its standards" it becomes "just another tool of human pride".'[11]

In contrast, Lovin argues that Niebuhr maintained that: 'It is the idea of One God which allows us to interpret human conflict in the light of an ultimate harmony of life with life, not the proximate experiences of harmony which require or permit us to posit an ultimate reality.'[12] This point leads naturally to the second dimension:

### Dimension 2: Morality

Moral obligation is not meaningless apart from God. Specific moral obligations that transcend immediate interests can be defined without reference to divine commands or an ultimate center of value. Rather, God provides a reality in which a comprehensive unity of moral meanings is conceivable. It makes sense to seek genuine harmony between persons and groups, rather than to manage their conflicts prudently or to surrender to superior force, because human aspirations and values can be unified by the value they have in relationship to God. This unity both completes and transcends the partial resolutions of differences we anticipate in nature and history, and it impels those who apprehend it in faith to seek forms of justice that go beyond present expectations, even when that search involves considerable risk to themselves. The reality of God means that love, and not prudence, is the law of life.[13]

Arguing that 'God provides a reality in which a comprehensive unity of moral meanings is conceivable' is clearly a form of moral realism, even moral objectivism. In terms of his notion of moral realism, Niebuhr argued both that ideology and self-interest constantly distort morality – for him sin often amounted to pride – and that viewed through the eyes of faith morality is ultimately grounded in harmony. There appears to be a double sense of 'realism' at work here: the first sceptical – ever conscious of sin and human finitude – and the second fideistic – maintaining that human understanding can be effectively moulded by Christian faith in a God of love.

---

[11] ibid., p. 54.
[12] ibid., p. 65.
[13] ibid., p. 67.

His notion of Christian moral realism also had a complex relationship to the Bible:

> Niebuhr thus weaves a complex relationship between Christian narrative and moral life. The uncompromising moral demands which Jesus makes in the Gospels are a necessary corrective to the shortcomings of rational ethics, which too easily becomes a justification of existing interests, rather than a motive to create new ways to resolve conflicts. But Jesus' ethics will not work for us in any simple way . . . To achieve the Social Gospel's goal of a transformed society, it is necessary to abandon the Social Gospel's stated purpose to apply Jesus' ethics directly to the problems of inequality, poverty, and social disorder.[14]

Despite this notion of moral realism Niebuhr is characteristically critical of natural law theory 'because, as he sees it, it reduces human cultures to determinate products of nature and ignores the large element of freedom and creativity in every social arrangement'.[15] Indeed a notion of human freedom which transcends given circumstances, and eventually transcends self too, is crucial to Niebuhr's morality. Once again faith is able to transcend and not simply to contradict the mundane. Lovin argues that this eminently Catholic position is actually quite close to those post-Vatican II concepts of natural law which are distinctly less tied to biology than were many natural law concepts in the past (Cahill and Porter both provide clear examples).

In *The Nature and Destiny of Man* Niebuhr argued that 'The vision of universal love . . . is relevant to all social relationships. For the limit of man makes it impossible to set limits of race, sex, or social condition upon the brotherhood that may be achieved in history.'[16] This quotation leads naturally to the final dimension.

### Dimension 3: Politics

Yet Niebuhr, who made his reputation as a political thinker by dissenting from the hopeful consensus of progressive

---

[14] ibid., p. 92.
[15] ibid., p. 122.
[16] Reinhold Niebuhr, *The Nature and Destiny of Man*, Vol. II, Scribners, New York, 1949, p. 85.

liberal optimism, remained in some ways a liberal in his own mature politics. Politics was for him an instrument of proximate goals, rather than ultimate commitments. He was interested in compromise and pragmatic choices, rather than in theological or ideological purity . . . For all his complaints about liberalism, especially in its post-Enlightenment forms, what he wanted, as he acknowledged late in his career, was a 'realistic liberalism' that would combine an appreciation of incremental gains in justice with a realistic assessment of the limits of reason and the power of tradition.[17]

Lovin argues that 'the Christian way of thinking about politics which Reinhold Niebuhr inherits from Augustine and Luther bears this suspicion of politics into modern times. Government represents a center of power that is necessary for order, but alien to faith'.[18] However Niebuhr takes this insight one step further: 'It is not only those who have evil intentions who need to be restrained if order is to be preserved. Those who intend only good, who want a society more just and more abundant than the one they know, may also have to be kept in check, lest they destroy what order does exist and then prove unable to replace it. Even those whose intentions are good may inflict tremendous suffering on others in their zeal to achieve their utopian visions.'[19] It is not difficult from this to see the negative side of Niebuhr's thoughts on politics or to see why he was quickly dubbed a political pessimist:

> The aim of Christian Realism is more than the check on evil and disorder that marked the limit of what Augustine and Luther expected from government. It is also more than the relentless criticism of the ideological self-deceptions of the powerful that Niebuhr regarded as a necessary complement to the power of the state. The aim is to make governments fully political, to allow individuals to give their visions institutional reality by enlisting the support of others, but also to transform those visions in the light of a more inclusive idea of freedom that emerges when persons are free to challenge, persuade, and criticize one another.[20]

[17] Lovin, op. cit., p. 160.
[18] ibid., p. 166.
[19] ibid., pp. 168–9.
[20] ibid., p. 189.

At the heart of Niebuhr's notion of politics is again a notion beyond politics – a transcending vision: 'People of faith who reject politics or ignore it not only leave the way open for the idolatries propagated by those of more limited vision. They also shut themselves off from a place in which they might meet the One true God.'[21] Indeed, in contrast to a facile utopianism, 'myths, utopias, and dreams of perfect justice provide the energy that keeps the struggle for justice going. They have the power to motivate people who would otherwise remain absorbed in the details of their personal struggles ... Persons and groups who nourish dreams of perfect justice make demands for specific, realizable approximations of their goal.'[22]

Interest in Niebuhr's writings seems to ebb and flow.[23] Whereas his vision and boldness often attract, his convolutions, lack of definitions and quixotic use of the Bible have tended to irritate. Robin Lovin's study helps considerably to rescue Niebuhr from his own weaknesses. Once Niebuhr's antagonism to a specifically theistic and modified use of natural law is dropped, some of his insights might yet be relevant to the post-MacIntyre debate in Christian ethics. Specifically in relation to the three levels of analysis that I identified in the previous chapter – legitimation, socialisation and institutionalisation – Reinhold Niebuhr's writings suggest important insights on the first two levels (his brother H. Richard Niebuhr was distinctly stronger on the third level).

At the level of legitimation, there are interesting links that can be made between Reinhold Niebuhr and Charles Taylor in his seminal *Sources of the Self*.[24] Both writers take pluralism/postmodernity seriously (albeit a generation apart) and yet remain inclusive in their approach to the secular world. Both are suspicious of forms of Christian exclusivism which deny that there are common human needs and goals – with Niebuhr rejecting the neo-orthodoxy that was popular earlier in the

[21] ibid., p. 190.
[22] ibid., p. 233.
[23] cf. Richard Harries (ed), *Reinhold Niebuhr and the Issues of Our Time*, Mowbrays, Oxford, 1986.
[24] Charles Taylor, *Sources of the Self: The Making of the Modern Identity*, CUP, Boston and Cambridge, 1989.

century and Taylor rejecting its radical postmodern versions today. For Niebuhr there are perennial human concerns about power and security, whereas for Taylor there are similar concerns about identity. Both are convinced that a theistic perspective sets limits to these concerns and helps individuals to transcend them. For Niebuhr seeing human conflicts in relation to God sets limits to these conflicts, whereas for Taylor a full account of human identity discloses that it has a framework which is most adequately understood in relation to God. Ironically both the Protestant Niebuhr and the Catholic Taylor are suspicious of natural law theories. Yet once it is realised that such theories are seldom considered plausible outside a context of theism, then perhaps their suspicion can be overcome. If one is already convinced that the world is created by a loving God, and one is not convinced that it is wholly overcome by sin, then it would seem reasonable to assume that traces of God's intentions will still be found in the natural realm (albeit subject to distortion). On this basis a theistic and modified account of natural law might be constructed using insights from writers such as Niebuhr and Taylor.

At the level of socialisation, there are interesting links that can be made between Niebuhr and MacIntyre. Both writers might accept that Christian values and virtues are shaped, sustained and carried primarily in Christian communities. Yet neither accepts the most radical postmodern position that communities of knowledge are incommensurable. On the contrary, both clearly gain insights from a variety of secular disciplines, whilst still believing that socialisation is primarily undertaken in particular communities. As a philosopher MacIntyre offers only broad hints about the distinctive features of Christian socialisation. Niebuhr, on the other hand, argues that the specifically Christian belief in a God of love can mould human understanding and finally transcend the mundane. However, in both writers there is also an important scepticism, not just about secular thought, but also about some of the pretensions of Christian theology. In contrast to the radical Christian postmodernists, Niebuhr, MacIntyre and indeed Taylor show a reticence in giving systematic accounts of distinctively Christian positions on moral and social issues. All three believe that it is only legitimate to depict values or virtues in tension in a manner which takes both Christian and secular resources seriously.

Of course, these are just hints. Their full development must be for a later date. Yet they suggest that Robin Lovin is indeed correct in thinking that Reinhold Niebuhr's writings have still much to offer. Lovin through Niebuhr gives a challenging glimpse of how the distinctiveness of Christian ethics might yet be defended even in a postmodern age.

# PART 2

༺✦༻

# FAITH AND FRAGMENTED FAMILIES

# 5

◄═┼═➤❊◄═┼═➤

# *The Changing Family and the Churches*

It is particularly in the area of the family and sexual relations that the moral challenge of postmodernity is most evident. Faced with a rapid decline in two-parent families, a rise in both teenage pregnancies and abortions, the awesome spread of AIDS, vociferous gay activism, and widespread confusion about the legal and social limits of pornography and obscenity, church leaders are currently facing an enormous challenge to what has often been regarded as their traditional teaching. If once Christian teaching might have appeared to be straight-forward in these areas – involving sexual intercourse only after marriage and life-long fidelity within marriage – today it is increasingly challenged both from outside and from within the churches.[1] In reality the ambiguities of sexuality have long been recognised at least in the pastoral practice of main-stream denominations. Nevertheless a perception of straight-forwardness in the past and only confusion in the present appears widespread.

Two physical changes do seem to have prompted these changes. The first of these, of course, is hormonal contra-ceptives, which have allowed women a degree of emancipation in the second half of the twentieth century without historical precedent. The second is a greatly increased life expectancy. Most couples who now marry in their late twenties can expect,

---

[1] For recent discussions see Adrian Thatcher and Elizabeth Stuart (eds), *Christian Perspectives on Sexuality and Gender*, Gracewing, Fowler Wright Books, Leominster, and Eerdmans, Grand Rapids, Michigan, 1996; and Stephen C. Barton (ed), *The Family in Theological Perspective*, T&T Clark, Edinburgh, 1996.

81

if they do not divorce, to celebrate their golden wedding. A comparative rarity in the past, could in the absence of divorce and/or cohabitation soon become commonplace. Yet these two physical changes hardly explain the whole of the radical shift in practice and attitudes that is currently taking place. Doubtless also driven by a combination of social and cultural factors – an increasingly globalised media, commercial pressures, political disenchantment, generational shifts, quite apart from postmodernity itself – people are changing fast and church leaders apparently find it increasingly difficult to know how to respond – not least because their own families are caught up in these changes.

Two recent Anglican reports attempt to cope honestly with these changes (honesty is not always a feature of church reports in this area). The first, *Something to Celebrate: Valuing Families in Church and Society*,[2] produced by a working party of the Church of England's Board for Social Responsibility, has already received widespread publicity in Britain. The second, *The Church and Human Sexuality*,[3] a much shorter report produced for the Anglican Church of the Province of South Africa, has not. Both reports attempt to face the changes that are taking place both outside and within the churches. Both value families with male and female biological parents raising their own children together. Both take the Bible seriously. Yet finally I suspect that the South Africans have something to teach the British. In the end, theirs is the report which is better sustained theologically.

In a trenchant review of *Something to Celebrate* Michael Banner argued in *Church Times*:

> There is no sustained engagement [in the report] with a Christian understanding of God – that is to say, there is no careful interrogation of the Bible, no diligent reflection on the doctrine of the Trinity, no dialogue with the rich tradition of Christian reflection on love and friendship, of which tradition the authors seem ignorant. In the end the working party nowhere displays the conviction that theology has anything decisively to contribute to our understanding of human

---

[2] Church House Publishing, 1995.
[3] Church of the Province of South Africa, 1995.

flourishing . . . And the recommendations to Church and nation with which the report ends include not a single one which the authors would have to withdraw if tomorrow they awoke to find themselves devoid of Christian faith. It is not, however, as far as we can tell, that the authors of the report don't believe in God, it is just that they don't seem to believe belief in God makes any difference.[4]

Coming after the very similar, although perhaps less abrasive, theological critiques made by such Christian ethicists as Duncan Forrester[5] and Nigel Biggar[6] of *Faith in the City*, and by myself[7] of *Faith in the Countryside*, it is surprising that the authors of *Something to Celebrate* did not heed these warnings. Theologians were always going to attack yet another Anglican report in which apparently the main thoughts and recommendations might equally have been made by sympathetic humanists.

It has already been emphasised in earlier chapters that Christian ethicists in a postmodern age are becoming increasingly concerned about distinctiveness. Whereas an earlier generation of Christian ethicists seemed to regard theological distinctiveness with suspicion – perhaps because they assumed that church and society were largely overlapping realities – a new generation views such distinctiveness as a *sine qua non* of the discipline. It is tempting to speculate that, had the membership responsible for any of these three reports contained more Christian ethicists, this distinctiveness might have emerged more clearly. Paradoxically, whilst Christian ethics now flourishes in the university and college worlds, it still languishes within many churches. Perhaps the latter assume too readily that church leaders are Christian ethicists simply by virtue of their office.

Yet Michael Banner's criticism is finally too harsh. Whilst he recognises that *Something to Celebrate* does contain biblical and theological reflection, he claims that it has made no substantive

---

[4] 'Nothing to Declare', *Church Times*, 16 June 1995, p. 7.

[5] Duncan B. Forrester, *Beliefs, Values and Politics*, Clarendon, Oxford, 1989, p. 84.

[6] Nigel Biggar, *Theological Politics: A Critique of 'Faith in the City'*, Latimer House Publications, Oxford, 1988.

[7] See my *Christian Ethics in Secular Worlds*, T&T Clark, Edinburgh, 1991, chapter 3.

difference to its main thoughts or conclusions – they could equally have been reached by a secular intelligentsia. However this verdict misses a crucial theological inheritance in the report – namely its stress upon the faithful two-parent family and upon marriage. Repeatedly the report stresses, as its subtitle clearly indicates, that it values families and marriage in church and society. In contrast, our secular intelligentsia is no longer so convinced. Increasingly it has concluded that the faithful two-parent family, let alone Christian marriage, is one of several viable options – a cohort convention, an arbitrary life-style choice – that and nothing more. Some radical feminists go further than this, viewing the two-parent family as amongst the most destructive of the options available. They are also deeply scathing about Jewish or Christian marriage and even more scathing about Islamic marriage.

There has, as Patricia Morgan has devastatingly shown in her *Farewell to the Family?*,[8] been a recent policy change in Britain, increasing income support for the lone parent at the expense of the two-parent family. She argues that, partly as a result of pressure from radical feminists, this shift of policy now means that in Britain, 'despite claims that the tax and benefit systems discriminate against lone parents, the lone parent receives more at every level of earnings than the married couple with children. The burden of taxation has increasingly been shifted onto married parents to the benefit of the single and the childless'.[9]

Interestingly, it was a theological dispute about the family which dominated some of the earlier meetings of the working party which produced *Something to Celebrate*. The dispute centred upon whether or not the New Testament supported the model of a two-parent family. It was argued that the stress upon celibacy in Paul, together with the Synoptic Jesus' apparently unmarried status and occasional caustic remarks about families, hardly amounted to a commendation of family life. Set in a Jewish context, the New Testament might appear almost anti-family – nuclear family or even extended family. Yet by the time

[8] Institute of Economic Affairs, London, 1995.
[9] ibid., p. 3.

the report had been completed a much more pro-family reading of the New Testament had triumphed. The section on the family in the Old Testament is slightly longer than that on the New, and that on the latter emphasises such features as Jesus' use of the Ten Commandments with their implicit assumptions about families.

The authors of *Something to Celebrate* believe, as a result specifically of their biblical studies, that Christians do have something distinctive to say which is different from society at large:

> What Christians believe Jesus to be calling for is quite radical in terms of contemporary social mores. It is the practice in marriage and family relationships of the kind of love which comes from God, a love which demands fidelity and commitment strong enough both to make the successful raising of children a realistic possibility and to undergird care and support through to old age.[10]

Even the much-publicised passages on cohabitation in *Something to Celebrate* are shaped by this theological commitment. Much press interest focused upon a single (and perhaps antiquated) paragraph which argued that 'the Church should . . . abandon the phrase "living in sin"'.[11] What was largely ignored was the statement two pages earlier that 'the wisest and most practical way forward . . . may be for Christians both to hold fast to the centrality of marriage and at the same time to accept that cohabitation is, for many people, a step along the way towards that fuller and more complex commitment'.[12] Whether one agrees with this statement or not, it is clear that has been shaped by a central commitment to marriage. This commitment, in turn, is rooted explicitly in theology, as the conclusion to the section on cohabitation makes clear:

> The Christian practice of lifelong, monogamous marriage lies at the heart of the Church's understanding of how the love of God is made manifest in the sexual companionship of a man and a woman. The increasing popularity of cohabitation,

---

[10] *Something to Celebrate*, p. 81.
[11] ibid., p. 117.
[12] ibid., p. 115.

among Christians and non-Christians, is no reason to modify this belief. On the contrary, it is an opportunity and a challenge to the Church to articulate its doctrine of marriage in ways so compelling, and to engage in a practice of marriage so life-enhancing, that the institution of marriage regains its centrality.[13]

These are not the words of secularity. Nevertheless they are perhaps too buried in the report. If a theologian such as Michael Banner can miss them, it is perhaps not surprising that others too, have identified this as yet another church report which baptizes a purely secular agenda.

The South African report is more careful to avoid such an impression. Unambiguously it starts with an extended biblical study of sexuality by the retired Rhodes University Professor of Theology, John Suggit. Although it is largely written in the biblical theology mode of a previous generation, it does succeed in identifying a number of biblical virtues that are held in tension on the issue of sexuality. Two sets of virtues are seen as particularly constant in both Old and New Testaments – loving-kindness/faithfulness on the one hand and righteousness/justice on the other. God's *hesed* or loving-kindness in the Old Testament is seen as continued in the New Testament in the form of *agape* and *charis* – all stressing the initiative of God's dealings with humans. Alongside this is a strong notion in both Testaments of *zedek*, of God's righteousness. Attempting to keep a balance between these two sets of virtues, the report offers three propositions in a descending order of God's relations to us and our relations to each other:

1. A Christian sexual ethic of love arises from faith's perception of God's ways with humankind in divine creativity and reconciliation, and in his action by which he sustains and liberates human beings so that they may live with justice (*zedek*) and integrity.

2. A sexual ethic centred in love needs to express mutual commitment between the partners, and to be liberating, enriching, honest, faithful, personally and socially responsible, life-giving and joyous.

[13] ibid., p. 118.

3. Love involves an attitude towards the other partner in which the happiness and welfare of the other is of prime importance, and which is expressed in appropriate acts. In view of the frequent distortion of sexuality by abusive power both within and outside marriage, a Christian sexual ethic is committed to the liberation of sexual expression as mutual enrichment rather than as dominance and submission.[14]

Having established this set of theological relations, the report then turns to evidence from biological and human sciences and concludes by examining the role of the churches. The results are not dramatically different from those of *Something to Celebrate*. Both are gentle and tolerant reports, fully aware of changes in society, wishing 'to be loving and neighbourly in the increasingly complex world of contemporary family and household life and . . . to be a source of hope and community in a world of alienation and anonymity'.[15] Neither report is prepared to be judgmental about faithful but active gay relationships or about cohabitation. In addition, the second report offers an understanding attitude towards brideprice, customary unions and polygamy – this is indeed an African report – and sees them in quite a different moral light to, for example, sexual promiscuity. The latter 'should be seen as a misunderstanding of the meaning of sexuality and a hindrance to the development of full human personality . . . as being opposed to God's will for human beings'.[16]

The fact that the South African report has a more explicitly theological beginning allows it to make rather clearer moral gradations later. By identifying at the outset a set of relevant theological virtues, it is able then to bring them to the various moral issues surrounding sexuality and families. In the light of a balance between loving faithfulness and righteousness, faithful and loving monogamy is seen as the Christian ideal for sexual sharing and with it for child raising. Other patterns of sexual sharing and child raising which form part of the complexity of African society – particularly customary marriage and polygamy – are seen as less than ideal but not as inherently opposed to

[14] *The Church and Human Sexuality*, para. B.4.
[15] *Something to Celebrate*, p. 209.
[16] *The Church and Human Sexuality*, para E.6.

this ideal. However, some prevalent forms of behaviour, such as sexual promiscuity, are indeed seen as inherently opposed to the ideal and thus as sinful.

Perhaps such a threefold pattern could allow church leaders in a postmodern age to show greater moral discernment in this confused and confusing area. *Something to Celebrate* could have been more helpful at this point. Starting from the same ideal as the South African report, the British report might have argued that alongside this ideal some prevalent forms of behaviour are indeed inherently opposed to it and are thus sinful – for example, promiscuity (both heterosexual and homosexual), adultery, prostitution, child pornography, active paedophilia and sado-masochism. Even though there are trends in secular society to legitimate all of these, on the basis of biblical virtues they remain sinful. However, there are other forms of behaviour which, in terms of these virtues, are not inherently sinful but which are still less than ideal. That is to say, they share some of the virtues without exemplifying them all. This group might contain patterns which are present 'in nature', such as child-lessness through spontaneous sterility, and others, such as faithful cohabitation, which are products more of culture. Faithful homosexual relationships may belong either to nature or to culture (morally that may not be too important since for both a homosexual orientation is not something an individual chooses). On this theological understanding, such relationships do indeed share some of the virtues of the Christian ideal.

Naturally there will still be disagreement amongst Christians about many of the vexed issues surrounding families and sexuality in a fast-changing world. That is only to be expected. However, an explicit theological agenda might at least help us to see more clearly how distinctively Christian decisions could be reached. We do not simply have to baptise every dominant but passing secular fantasy.

# 6

# *'Veritatis Splendor'*

### *An Initial Response*

Perhaps it was to be expected. *Veritatis Splendor* has been judged before being properly read. 'This is merely John-Paul II re-asserting the conservative teaching on contraception of *Humanae Vitae*' was one immediate reaction. 'This is simply an ageing Pope reclaiming his authority' was another.

We may have missed the real significance of this encyclical. What it offers is an astute analysis of some of the intellectual weaknesses of modern culture. It also asserts that matters of right and wrong really do have an objective basis. Values are not simply matters of passing opinion. Without accepting all of its conclusions, Christians of many different persuasions might benefit from the central thrust of this important encyclical.

One of the Pope's sharpest observations is this. Individual conscience and autonomy have become ever more important in ethics at precisely the moment when genetic and social determinism have also come into vogue. Put bluntly, we are constantly told today that it should be for the individual alone to decide between right and wrong. Society at large should not moralise. And then in the next breath we are told that none of us is actually free to make serious choices – all is coded by our genes or determined by social factors.

Again, we are often told that matters of right and wrong are always relative. We cannot instruct others in morality. Everyone must work out their morality on their own. In the next breath again we are told that the destruction of the environment, or the torture of animals and people, are self-evidently wrong.

Moral outrage continues even in the midst of moral relativism. If we cannot see that the Holocaust is wrong we are moral degenerates. But if we think that certain types of sexual activity are wrong we are moral prudes.

Such moral inconsistencies abound in Western culture today and yet they go largely unchallenged. It is to the great credit of *Veritatis Splendor* that it does challenge them. Perhaps it is one of the advantages of being a Pope not to feel bound to produce a teaching document that is founded on consensus. Instead of a balanced report – which gives full credit to conflicting views and then seeks a tentative compromise between them – the Pope offers forceful teaching.

Of course, on particular issues this can be deeply distressing for individual Roman Catholics. The issue of 'artificial' contraception remains a thorn in the side of many young Catholics. Yet on a broader canvas, the Pope is able to address the large issues with force and conviction in a way that few others can.

Perhaps the largest issue – reflected in the title of the encyclical – is that of truth. The Pope argues that it is truth which is now one of the greatest casualties of Western culture in the area of morality. Individual freedom and personal autonomy are elevated to an absolute status. What individuals do with their freedom and autonomy is entirely up to them. In the process 'to the affirmation that one has a duty to follow one's conscience is unduly added the affirmation that one's moral judgment is true merely by the fact that it has its origin in the conscience'.

Such solipsism leaves us at the mercy of some very strange consciences. Doubtless Peter Sutcliffe or David Koresh acted in the light of their consciences. Truth simply goes by the board. 'Once the idea of a universal truth about the good, knowable by human reason, is lost, inevitably the notion of conscience also changes . . . Taken to its extreme consequences, this individualism leads to a denial of the very idea of human nature.'

The Pope even detects a link between certain understandings of democracy and moral relativism. The mediaeval Aquinas was altogether suspicious of democracy – but then for him the term denoted quite literally 'mob rule'. What I suspect disturbs the Pope today is the idea that moral issues should simply be decided by plebiscite or by its modern counterpart, the opinion poll. In effect this holds that we should do what most people currently think we should do. Notoriously this is the path to retribution and discrimination against unpopular minorities. Yet on many moral issues it is the path that is most frequently espoused.

There is, I believe, an important distinction which should be made at this point – between relativism as a method and relativism as an article of faith. The two easily slip into each other, but it is always a mistake to confuse them. It is properly the job of the social scientist to examine everything – including moral beliefs and practices – in social terms. Yet it is a foolish social scientist who then imagines that this method exhausts the meaning of these beliefs and practices. Social science, in the process, is simply transformed from a method into an article of faith.

A number of physical scientists have recently made a similar jump. For example, it is indeed the job of the geneticist to explain human nature in genetic terms. But science becomes a sort of religion if the geneticist then presumes from this that there is nothing else to human nature but our genetic codes. Science as religion is quite a frightening spectacle – if science is the only path to human knowledge, then who is to protect us from the products of science? When challenged at a televised Oxford debate to 'explain' Mozart exhaustively in genetic terms, Richard Dawkins responded simply by claiming that in time geneticists would be able to do so. A very clear declaration of faith on his part!

Against such confused assumptions, *Veritatis Splendor* upholds a traditional understanding of natural law. Conscience is not simply a dialogue with oneself, it is also a dialogue between oneself and God. For the Christian there is an intimate connection between conscience and prayer. And what is right and wrong is not simply a matter of idiosyncratic personal opinion; it is connected with the way that God has created the universe.

Through reason – so long as it is not distorted by sin and self-interest – individuals can have access to moral precepts. 'At the heart of the moral life we thus find the principle of a "rightful autonomy" of man, the personal subject of his actions. The moral law has its origin in God and always finds its source in him: at the same time, by virtue of natural reason, which derives from divine wisdom, it is properly human law . . . man possesses in himself his own law, received from the Creator'.

Of course, some Christians, following Calvin and others, have argued that human nature, apart from Christ, is so totally depraved that it is no longer possible to glimpse anything of the Creator's intention within it. This is a logical position, but it pays a heavy price for its logic. Any apparent manifestations of goodness in the secular world must simply be treated as illusions. And other faiths must always be thoroughly patronised – they may think that they have discerned something about God, but they must simply be wrong.

If Christians avoid such a position, then I believe that they do have something to learn from *Veritatis Splendor*. If we believe in a loving Creator, then it does seem reasonable to believe that this Creator has left images of goodness in human nature. So when secular relativists express deep moral outrage at injustice in the world, the believer will naturally see this as such an image. For the believer it is a part of the undeclared faith of an apparently secular world. Furthermore, perhaps it is the business of the theologian to make such undeclared faith more manifest. That is exactly what *Veritatis Splendor* attempts to do. Perhaps it could be the most crucial role for theology in the next century.

Of course, *Veritatis Splendor* does not resolve all of the problems of method facing Christian ethics. As the Archbishop of York acutely observes elsewhere in *Church Times*, there has been a tendency for the natural law tradition to view human nature in too static terms. Nature as a whole evolves and becomes in a way that was unsuspected by Aquinas. However, I suspect that the tradition can cope with this observation without succumbing to the moral relativism which the Pope so strongly attacks.

Again, a besetting weakness of the natural law tradition has been to mistake current prejudices for unchanging features of the natural order. It should never be forgotten that Aquinas regarded slavery as 'natural' and women as by nature less rational than men. Perhaps John-Paul II too, has his prejudices. Many Western Catholics believe that he has, especially in the area of contraception.

Finally, the encyclical is unlikely to make many converts amongst secularists. It is steeped in quotations from the Bible and its notion of natural law, although accessible to reason, does presume a Creator. It offers no secular rationale for the natural law tradition. Frankly I doubt if such a rationale is possible. Yet what is possible is a much more proactive critique of dominant secular assumptions about morality from a Christian perspective. And that the encyclical does 'splendidly'.

## A Later Review

When *Veritatis Splendor* was published in August 1993 a number of people in the media were immediately perplexed. They had expected a straightforward reassertion of conservative teaching on contraception. What they got instead was a rather moving Bible study on the story of the rich young man, an impassioned defence of martyrdom, and resting between the two a detailed analysis and critique of social relativism and moral theory in intellectual culture today. A rigorist position on contraception was mentioned, but only in passing. Decoding this unusual mixture has required the help of some sharp theological minds. Pure journalism could not cope.

Two subsequent books are useful in helping this process of decoding.[1] Of the two the SPCK collection is the more distinguished, the less expensive, and it contains the full text of *Veritatis Splendor* as a bonus. However, there are useful essays in both collections.[2] The SPCK articles were first published in *The Tablet*, whose editor supplies a clear and helpful introduction. They were written mainly by American and British Roman Catholic theologians (most of them opposed in varying degrees to the encyclical) and by the Anglican Oliver

[1] John Wilkins (ed), *Understanding Veritatis Splendor: The Encyclical Letter of Pope John Paul II on the Church's Moral Teaching*, SPCK, London, 1994; and Charles Yeats (ed), *Veritatis Splendor: A Response by Twelve Contributors*, Canterbury Press, Norwich, 1994.

[2] See also the useful reviews in *Studies in Christian Ethics*, Vol. 7, No. 2.

O'Donovan. The Canterbury Press collection is a predominantly Anglican product consisting of invited sermons and lectures first given at Durham.

When the encyclical was first published I argued that one of its sharpest observations was that in the secular world individual conscience and autonomy have become ever more important at precisely the moment when genetic and social determinism have also become more predominant. Few of the contributors to either collection give sufficient credit to the Pope for this sharp wisdom. Many do acknowledge his proper role in challenging secular relativism – now that the secular dogmatism of communism has collapsed – and express some admiration for his courage in doing so. Yet they still give him less credit than I believe he deserves for his observations about the sheer inconsistencies of many secular moral assumptions.

Many of the Catholic authors in the SPCK collection are concerned above all else to identify the targets that the Pope has in mind within the church rather than within the secular world. But perhaps the Pope is himself to blame for this. As Nicholas Lash argues, if he had simply identified the church's agenda in challenging the secular world, instead of also taking sideswipes at his own unnamed moral theologians, this would have been a much more impressive encyclical altogether. As a result of these side-swipes, Bernhard Häring, Richard McCormick and Herbert McCabe all produce impressive counter-attacks to the encyclical.

An interesting point of contact between the two collections is the feminist contributions of Lisa Sowle Cahill to the SPCK book and Ann Loades to the Canterbury Press book. Cahill mounts a gentle, but finally devastating, feminist critique of *Veritatis Splendor*.[3] As a Catholic she does wish to affirm a connection between embodiment and love in sexuality. However as a woman she is deeply conscious of the male presumptions that she sees in the encyclical – the stress upon authority, the male language, the aggression towards forms of Christian ethics other than the Pope's own, the location of artificial

---

[3] See also her *Sex, Gender and Christian Ethics*, CUP, Cambridge and New York, 1996.

contraception (and indeed most forms of fertility treatment) in a negative and rule-based frame. The virtues of compassion and care are seldom at the fore-front. Loades concurs. To Cahill's reaction she adds an Anglican feminist response which is still sympathetic to some of the major concerns of the Pope. Although she is by no means an absolutist she still finds herself 'to be profoundly uneasy when I try to think about a society such as ours in which we now have, apparently, some 180,000 abortions a year'.

Autonomy and private conscience cannot be adequate arbiters of morality in society today. Yet bioethics seems to be increasingly convinced that they are. Thank God the Pope has the courage to challenge this. How sad he chose to offer this challenge in a way that was bound to anger his own moral theologians.

# 7

⇒+✠+⇐

# 'Evangelium Vitae'

### An Initial Response

Western democracies are slowly becoming aware of a massive moral problem. In his latest encyclical, *Evangelium Vitae* or *The Gospel of Life*, Pope John-Paul II has once again located this problem in a trenchant manner. Having done so much to dismantle Eastern Communism, he yet remains a fierce moral critic of Western democracy.

The moral problem can be expressed quite simply. In a democracy, how can individual freedoms not degenerate into general licence? How can liberties supported by a majority of people avoid becoming rights for all but with no correlative duties? How can a process of moral liberalisation not lead eventually to a state of moral anarchy? Why allow individuals an ever increasing amount of personal autonomy and choice, when they are less and less clear about how any moral choices can be made?

In short, Western democracy allows ever greater moral freedom whilst simultaneously deconstructing all moral guidelines and authorities.

The Roman Catholic Church is not exactly the most democratic of churches. Neither is the present Pope the most democratic of popes. In his new encyclical he argues that political democracy is a means not an end. He is unimpressed with the idea that what is morally right should be equated with what most people at the moment desire. He even disputes the idea that 'the legal system of any society should limit itself to taking into account of and accepting the conviction of the majority'.

For him this is the route to 'the ethical relativism which char-
acterizes much of present-day culture'. In contrast, he argues
forcefully that there are moral truths, whether most people can
perceive them or not. He believes that culture can become
misdirected, even evil and that, in some respects, Western
democracy is indeed misdirected, even evil. He is emphatic that
'democracy cannot be idolized to the point of making it a sub-
stitute for morality or a panacea for immorality'.

So far there is much in common here with his very important
1993 encyclical *Veritatis Splendor*. There he was deeply scathing
of both social determinism and ethical relativism and emphatic
that there is such a thing as 'truth' on moral issues. What has
happened in Western culture, he argued in 1993, is that 'the
inescapable claims of truth disappear, yielding their place to a
criterion of sincerity, authenticity and "being at peace with
oneself", so much so that some have come to adopt a radically
subjectivistic conception of moral judgment'.

In his new encyclical the Pope extends this polemic against
modern Western culture and gives it two new twists. The first,
and the most surprising, is the apocalyptic tone that he now
adopts. Repeatedly he calls modern culture a 'culture of death'.
There is a new urgency here: 'today this proclamation is
especially pressing because of the extraordinary increase and
gravity of threats to the life of individuals and peoples,
especially where life is weak and defenceless'. The second twist
shows the reason for this. Whereas *Veritatis Splendor* offered
a general argument with few particulars, *Evangelium Vitae*
offers direct and polemical teaching on bioethics and sexuality.
It is a fearless document offering few comforts to modern
culture and challenging a growing secular consensus at almost
every point.

The Pope is particularly concerned that first abortion and
now direct forms of euthanasia become legalised in Western
democracies and that, as a result, these democracies will
increasingly resemble 'cultures of death'. At stake is the issue of
'respect for life'. He argues passionately that respect for human
life is a fundamental right based firmly upon natural law. It is
strictly non-negotiable whatever the will of democratically
expressed majorities. Indeed he sees a deep irony in attempts to

legalise abortion and direct euthanasia: 'precisely in an age
when the inviolable rights of the person are solemnly pro-
claimed and the value of life is publicly affirmed, the very right
to life is being denied or trampled upon, especially at the more
significant moments of existence: the moment of birth and the
moment of death'.

Why the urgency and why the apocalyptic language? There
can be little doubt that it is actual euthanasia in Holland,
proposed and actual euthanasia legislation in several countries,
and the pressure towards legalisation in many more, that has
goaded the Pope. The campaign to halt legalised abortion was
lost in the 1960s. The campaign to legalise direct euthanasia
(voluntary and indeed involuntary) is now fully under way. The
Pope is surely attempting to make a pre-emptive strike, whilst
in effect admitting that the 'culture of death' is already
becoming well established.

In passing he also restates his well known opposition to
'artificial' contraception, to *in vitro* fertility treatments, to sexual
laxity and to suicide. He sees them all as linked to a 'culture of
death': since 'such practices are rooted in a hedonistic mentality
unwilling to accept responsibility in matters of sexuality, and
they imply a self-centred concept of freedom, which regards
procreation as an obstacle to personal fulfilment'. Even *in vitro*
fertility treatments tend to contribute to this mentality, since
they separate procreation from sexual intercourse and then
finally destroy 'spare' embryos. Such a 'culture of death' in effect
excludes God. In an increasingly secular world 'when the sense
of God is lost, there is also a tendency to lose the sense of man,
of his dignity and his life; in turn, the systematic violation of
the moral law, especially in the serious matter of respect for
human life and its dignity, produces a kind of progressive
darkening of the capacity to discern God's living and saving
presence'.

What are other Christians to make of this? This is an
extraordinarily impassioned encyclical. The Pope has become
a prophet in old age. He has dropped the even tones of
some of his earlier encyclicals and has adopted instead the
apocalyptic tones of urgency and denunciation. Direct involuntary euthanasia is simply termed 'murder'; both procured

abortion and direct euthanasia in any form are denounced as 'absolutely unacceptable'; and doctors who perform them are described as 'agents of death'. And women who have had an abortion are chillingly told to seek 'forgiveness from your child, who is now living in the Lord'. Prophets seldom court popularity.

Prophets also have a tendency to exaggerate. Most non-Catholic Christians (and indeed most married Roman Catholics in the West) do not believe that hormonal and barrier forms of contraception have engendered a 'culture of death' in their own lives. Most, I suspect, will be unhappy about his blunt rejection of *in vitro* fertility treatments for couples who are desperate to have children and will often make splendid parents. Many of us have agonised long and hard about abortion and still believe that it can be justified, even if we deplore its casual use for life-style reasons. And on the issue of euthanasia the Pope raises almost as many problems as he resolves. He does allow for the withdrawal of invasive treatment on the terminally ill and for the giving of analgesics which might shorten life. But he does not tell us how to resolve the dilemmas created by persistent vegetative state patients (the next section will return to this issue) or when indirect treatment becomes direct euthanasia.

Yet having made such caveats there is still much force in this encyclical. It does highlight the central problem with which I started. Few religious leaders in Britain – apart from the splendid Jonathan Sacks – have identified it so clearly. It can be illustrated quite simply. Those of us who supported a change in the abortion law in the 1960s on compassionate grounds did not realise at the time how quickly a liberty would be turned into a right. In the first trimester of pregnancy we now effectively have abortion on demand in Britain. When we campaigned for effective contraception and women's rights, we did not realise that by the 1990s one-in-three children would be born outside marriage and that one-in-five would be brought up by a woman on her own. The much vilified encyclical *Humane Vitae* did warn us back in 1968 that 'marital infidelity and a general lowering of moral standards' would result from the dissemination of new forms of contraception, and that a woman would be reduced by a man 'to being a mere instrument for the satisfaction of his own desires, no longer considering her as his partner whom he should surround with care and affection'.

Might not something similar be about to happen with direct euthanasia? It will doubtless be introduced for the most compassionate of reasons. Newspapers are already presenting a succession of tragic cases which seem to justify direct intervention. But, once legalised, what is to stop it becoming a right for all and then a tyranny against the weak and the powerless?

The Pope does have a point. I am glad that I do not have to obey him. Yet he does make me think.

# 8

## Jonathan Sacks' 'Faith in the Future'

### A Review

Even in a postmodern age morality can be a bridge. Morality may indeed offer religious leaders today their most important public voice. Surprisingly in a confused society, morality is increasingly regarded as important and religious traditions are still considered to be relevant to it.

I have a running joke with secular philosophy colleagues in my University. They sometimes tease me that I have no rational grounds for my belief in God. In turn I tease them that they have no rational grounds for their moral beliefs – they rely instead upon borrowed Judaeo-Christian values. Neither of these claims is completely true, but they have enough force for both parties to call for a temporary truce.

In a secular university a modern theologian, who is clearly identified with a faith tradition, still has a public role precisely because values are thought to be important. Current moral confusion enhances this role. The special authority of Jonathan Sacks is that he is one of the few religious leaders in Britain today to have identified this public role. A trained philosopher, well read in sociology, and with the rare skills of an articulate communicator, he is also a figure of faith, firmly but inclusively and even romantically rooted in Orthodox Judaism. These are powerful combinations for a morally confused society.

He established a national reputation with his 1990 Reith Lectures, *The Persistence of Faith*.[1] A decade earlier Edward

[1] Jonathan Sacks, *The Persistence of Faith*, Weidenfeld & Nicholson, London, 1992.

Norman had gained a reputation from his Reith Lectures[2] for being a sharp critic of his own faith tradition. Jonathan Sacks instead commanded respect for commending religious faith as a challenge to secularism. Ironically it was the Orthodox Jew, not the traditionalist Christian, who appeared as the apologist for a persisting faith.

In *The Persistence of Faith* Jonathan Sacks argued strongly against the claims of secular pluralism. He noted that religious communities – whether Jewish, Christian or Islamic – are often expected to abandon their distinctiveness in the modern world in the name of some higher humanism. In contrast he sought to defend a critical understanding of orthodoxy as a mid-path between liberalism and fundamentalism:

> For the past century religion has been embattled and defensive. This has led to the two religious stances most common in the modern world, a diffuse liberalism on the one hand, sanctifying secular trends after the event; and a reactive extremism on the other, willing us back into a golden age that neither was nor will be again. The two live by their sibling rivalries, each seeing the other as the main threat to salvation.[3]

The path of critical orthodoxy, in contrast, offers a real challenge to modern secularity. It suggests that 'faith persists and in persisting allows us to build a world more human than one in which men, nations or economic systems have become gods. Twenty years ago it seemed as if religion had run its course in the modern world. Today a more considered view would be that its story has hardly yet begun.'

In his new book, *Faith in the Future*,[4] he returns to these themes and applies them in a very practical way to some of the dilemmas of the late twentieth century – one-parent families, the loss of community, urban despair, lawlessness, the loss of collective traditions and myths. Above all he argues that we are losing hope – hope in the future – hope which 'is born and has its being in the context of family, community and religious faith'.

[2] Edward Norman, *Christianity and the World Order*, OUP, Oxford, 1979.
[3] Sacks, op. cit., p. 94.
[4] Jonathan Sacks, *Faith in the Future*, Darton, Longman & Todd, London, 1995.

Jonathan Sacks' strength as an Orthodox Jew is that he regards this triumvirate – family, community and faith – as the bed-rock of society. He is appalled by a society in which one in three children are born outside of marriage and in which one in five children are brought up by single parents (usually women). For him this breakdown of family contributes sharply to the loss of community and, with it, to a loss of faith. Families enhance the well-being of society. Families, in turn, are nurtured by tradition and foster faith. He uses repeated examples from his own family experience of ways in which the Jewish sabbath and festivals penetrate and sustain lives. Built around a common pattern and faith such families have been able to withstand even the appalling tragedies that have so often confronted Judaism. As an Orthodox Jew, Jonathan Sacks seeks to trace the web of links from families, through communities and out to society at large. For him these are essential links.

Few Christians today can write with such obvious power and conviction. We have become more confused and/or less convincing about these links. We find it difficult to defend the family intelligently, let alone articulate a coherent concept of moral communities or identify the distinctive contributions of faith in a pluralistic world. Jonathan Sacks even comes to the aid of Christians at several points. Politicians and media producers might expect his support as a Jew as they dismantle what they see as privileged Christian provisions – whether a closed period for religion on television or a ban on Sunday trading. Instead he argues that changes in these areas have been driven more by secularism than by a desire for religious freedom.

Although he shares many concerns with the present Pope, there is none of the apocalyptic language of *Evangelium Vitae* here. Both religious leaders are powerful critics of the implicit assumptions of modernity – especially of claims to individual 'autonomy' and 'rights' without any corresponding notion of 'responsibilities' and 'inter-dependence'. Both defend monogamous, faithful family life. Both are steeped in their respective faith traditions. However Jonathan Sacks' voice is finally the more inclusive and less shrill.

Of course, there are weaknesses in his writings. As an Orthodox Jew he is largely silent about Reformed Jews – even referring to a book by my colleague, Rabbi Dan Cohn-Sherbok, whilst omitting mention of his name. Again he recounts the views, for example, of the ultra-Orthodox on the Holocaust, whilst not telling us whether or not he holds these views himself. He repeatedly uses Scripture but seldom makes direct use of the critical scholarship of that Scripture. In short, he has a tendency to run with the fox and hunt with the hounds. Perhaps that is how he manages to remain both Chief Rabbi and a figure of such interest to the secular media. Deeply interesting, but also enigmatic and elusive.

# PART 3

# CONTENTIOUS MORAL ISSUES

# 9

✂︎✦︎✂︎

# Values and
# Church Management

Following publication of the *Working as One Body: The Report of the Archbishops' Commission on the Organisation of the Church of England*[1] – more commonly called the Turnbull Report – there has been considerable discussion about the appropriateness of churches using new management concepts. Of course, the moral discussion about the 'new management culture' extends considerably beyond the churches – it now affects many areas of life in a postmodern age. This chapter will examine three connected theses (each of which can be extended beyond the churches): that the adoption of new management concepts by church leaders is more to do with technique than with ideology; that the predominant management concepts in churches based upon consensus, professional autonomy and incremental budgets, contain some serious moral flaws; and that new management concepts, far from being secular importations into churches, instead have theological roots.

### Technique Rather Than Ideology

Earlier I promised to return to moral issues raised by the book that Derek Burke and I wrote recently, *Strategic Church Leadership*.[2] In this we argued that management and strategic planning concepts are more to do with technique than with ideology. Of course, we were aware that many professionals,

---

[1] Church House, London, 1995.
[2] SPCK, London, 1996.

particularly within the churches, universities and health services, disagree strongly with this position. We illustrated this disagreement with quotations first by Eric Kemp, Bishop of Chichester, and second by Nigel McCulloch, Bishop of Wakefield. Writing in *Church Times*, the first responded as follows to the Turnbull Report:

> What the Commission says about staff should be carefully scrutinised. Phrases such as 'a single unified staff, developing a coherence and singleness of purpose', and 'staff must be given freedom to manage, and more responsibility and accountability for directing the outcome of their work', ring alarm bells about the approach of Sir Humphrey and the Civil Service. These things may be appropriate in the financial and business world. I doubt whether they are so over the whole range of the Church's life . . . In the end, the question is whether what is suitable and appropriate for a business organisation is equally suitable and appropriate for all aspects of the life of the Body of Christ.[3]

We noted that the argument here derives its force from an assumption that 'management' and the business world are alien worlds to the churches. The other quotation, this time from Nigel McCulloch, appeared in his diocesan newsletter just before the Turnbull Report was published:

> There is absolutely no doubting the fact that, in the increasingly difficult tasks clergy are facing, as much pastoral support as possible is needed. But I am not at all sure that systematic appraisal and review is coterminous with good pastoral care. What deeply worries me is the way in which, often uncritically, we are adopting too many of the assumptions and techniques of modern management. That is not to deny that there are some good ideas from the secular world which the church could adapt, and indeed does, with advantage. But, increasingly I am persuaded that the proper context for reviewing and developing ministry ought not to be quasi-management but spiritual direction. Indeed, if appraisal and review are not chiefly a spiritual matter then something is wrong. Most problems in our church life and our personal life, whether we are lay or ordained, are spiritual problems. A good

[3] *Church Times*, 17 November 1995.

spiritual director will understand enough psychology to appreciate different personality traits – and be able to give wise advice, based not only on knowledge but his or her own depth of spirituality. Furthermore, a spiritual director is not going to put things on files – so, for clergy especially, there is a huge release and opportunity for frankness and honesty which are unlikely in a hierarchical, and even a peer, system. But, even more important, placing this firmly within spiritual direction avoids the growing problem of answerability to those who increasingly pay the stipend. The inevitable blunting of prophetic ministry and the narrowing of mission outreach is a very disturbing feature of certain free churches where the elders insist: 'we pay you – so you must do and say what we wish'.[4]

In response we conceded that management and strategic leadership theory adopted uncritically and thoughtlessly can indeed be extremely damaging. For example, teaching audits in universities, which concentrate exclusively upon techniques and ignore the actual substance of what is taught, can be deeply misleading. But we also noted that amongst an increasing number of management theorists there is now a recognition that institutions can over plan and become too rigid. Henry Mintzberg's striking book *The Rise and Fall of Strategic Planning*[5] argues that institutions do need to remain flexible, to respond imaginatively to unexpected changes, and to be open to creative visions. Nevertheless, effective teaching does still have to give some attention to such issues as library resources, bibliographies, audibility, intelligibility to the listeners, as well as to student feed-back and to review procedures. Mintzberg himself concludes that 'too much planning may lead us to chaos, but so too would too little, and more directly'.[6] A similar case might, we believe, be made out for the churches too. Whilst theological and spiritual considerations should be their starting point, this does not excuse them from careful planning and use of resources.

The Turnbull Report, of course, is also emphatic that theology must be the driving force of change within churches:

[4] *Wakefield Diocesan Newsletter: See-Link*, March 1995.
[5] Prentice Hall, New York, 1994.
[6] p. 416.

'the chief resource of the Church is the grace of God. No amount of structure and organisation can "put the Church right" if, at every level, it is not turning to God for his provision'.[7] Yet, whilst a theological agenda is crucial for the authors of the report, it is not exhaustive. It provides the direction in which ministry should go, but it does not provide the means for checking whether or not this has been achieved effectively, that is for monitoring outcomes. So, 'spiritual direction' might well ensure that individual ministers are properly motivated. What it will not ensure is that they are also effective and contributing creatively to the church as a whole. What must, for example, a church with a declining budget keep and what must it let go? Spiritual direction as such will not help here, but a clear sense of priorities, firmly based upon theology, might.

It was at this point that we argued that one way of coping with this criticism of management theories is to emphasise that these are techniques and not ideology. Of course, they can be turned into an ideology – and perhaps that is Bishop Nigel McCulloch's worry – but that is not usually the intention of the more sophisticated management theorists. Mintzberg sets out at great length the disasters that can befall institutions which adopt a slavish approach to strategic planning. Business leaders who treat strategic plans almost as if they are creeds soon come to believe that everything can be pre-determined, that all outcomes can be accurately forecast, and that forecasting is a form of 'magic'. Ironically such a credal approach to strategic planning was often adopted in the Soviet Union before 1989: 'they controlled everything in their plans except the weather. Nature intervened, the crops failed, and the plan was thrown into turmoil.'[8] On this understanding, strategic planning should properly be regarded as technique not as creed.

We also noted that Nigel McCulloch's criticism of the Free Churches – talking about 'the growing problem of answerability to those who increasingly pay the stipend' – was typical of a leader in a heavily subsidised church. In *The Myth of the*

---

[7] para. 2.19.
[8] p. 239.

*Empty Church*[9] I argued at length that subsidy has in fact deeply misled the Church of England. It has for long given some of its clergy the impression that they can be more 'prophetic' than Free Church ministers. In reality in the nineteenth century, when prophetic ministry was both common and effective (especially amongst socially conscious Evangelicals), it was some of the entrepreneurial Free Churches which were the more prophetic. The Church of England, by comparison, resolutely tended to defend the status quo on moral and political issues. Subsidy also allowed the Church of England to maintain church structures which contributed directly to numerical decline. Far from economic subsidy freeing the Church of England to engage in mission outreach, it tended to cushion many of its clergy from any impetus towards such outreach. In effect it allowed clergy to be paid whether or not they were engaged in mission outreach and whether or not they had effective congregations. In contrast, a clearer connection between payment and answerability has been an important factor allowing American churches to flourish whilst their British and European counterparts have tended to decline.

## Is 'Consensus' Without Moral Defects?

But are recent management theories and strategic planning really technique and not ideology? It is often argued that recent management practices contain deep moral failings and that strategic planning is simply too ruthless for church leaders. It is frequently maintained that churches should not replicate the faults of the current management culture. Chronic job in-security, obsession with budgets, oversimplistic singlemindedness, undervaluing of supposedly 'unproductive' colleagues, viewing people solely in terms of their market worth, and reducing everything to measurable outcomes, are only some of the faults that are seen in this management culture. It is not the business of churches, so many argue, to surrender to this alien culture. Churches should continue to witness to the

[9] SPCK, London, 1993.

virtues of consensus, harmony, non-measurable qualities, and full employment.

Richard Roberts has provided a powerful critique of the Turnbull Report on precisely these grounds. He argues:

> Central to the Report is a vision of the Church as an executive-led, highly unified organisation, in many respects similar to a business corporation. There will in effect be a World President (the Archbishop of Canterbury), a Company Chairman (again the Archbishop of Canterbury), an Executive Board (the proposed National Council of senior bishops and appointees) and a Chief Executive with considerable powers (the Secretary General) and many key, leading positions will be occupied by archiepiscopal appointees. Part of the plan involves the effective subordination of other important bodies to the Executive. Most notably, General Synod will become an advisory and legislative body representative of other stakeholders, which will, rather like periodic meetings of shareholders keep the Executive in indirect contact with wider realities.[10]

The central thrust of this analysis is altered little by the General Synod's attempts to have more elected members on the central board. Roberts insists that Turnbull replaces consensus and autonomy with a hierarchical executive which 'involves sophisticated means of enforcement'. Thus:

> Managerial enforcement involves a highly differentiated process of de-skilling and the gradual stripping away of professional autonomy from middle-ranking employees. For the latter, the application of British Standard 5750 and ISO 9000 in Quality Audit involves the devising of intricate, self-imposed and internalised patterns of obediential behaviour. For the lower ranks control is simply external and regulatory and the desired effects achieved through the behaviourist training schemes perfected in 'McDonaldised' systems of product and service delivery.[11]

There is an element of *reductio ad absurdum* in Roberts' argument. The very limited notion of accountability in the Turnbull Report (only the reduced role of the Church Commissioners is analysed in terms of accountability) hardly

---

[10] *New Directions*, General Synod, January 1996, p. 5.
[11] ibid.

amounts to the rigorous manufacturing audit procedures of British Standard 5750. Certainly there is nothing remotely present to match his claim that 'no doubt learning rapidly from practitioners in other commercial, business and service organisations, there will be those who will build their careers on the basis of implementing the ecclesial equivalents of performance indicators, Quality Audit, Pew Customer Charters, and so on; besides making sure that the church's version of "company loyalty" gently but surely stifles all dissentient voices'.[12] Nonetheless, Roberts' defence of professional autonomy and his suspicion of centralised 'enforcement' may well be shared by others.

But are the values of consensus, professional autonomy and equitable incrementality quite as unassailable as some imagine? It can be argued that professional autonomy linked to consensus decision-making, which has been such a crucial feature of synodical government in the Church of England over the last quarter century, has actually proved to be a serious impediment to change. On a number of crucial issues – such as ecumenical unions and covenants, the marriage of divorcees in church, and until recently the ordination of women – the will of the majority in the Church of England has been thwarted for many years. Minorities, usually clerical minorities, soon discovered that the General Synod gave them a powerful veto to resist change whatever the majority of other churchpeople wanted. In *Strategic Church Leadership* we argue that consensus leadership has also tended to stunt the missionary role of the Church of England. Those clergy who have no interest in mission, and who regard the numbers of people coming to public worship as irrelevant, have an equal say with those who do believe in mission and are deeply concerned about numbers. In effect, Roberts' 'dissentient voices' prevail.

The negative features of the present system of professional autonomy are also recognised by the Turnbull Report:

> The Church's management of its human resources – its most precious resource – is characterised by an incoherence in policy aggravated by confused structures. In relation to the ordained

[12] ibid.

ministry, for example, there is no single plan for the optimum numbers needed and how they are to be trained and deployed, and for making the necessary financial projections and plans for how the costs of their stipends and pensions are to be met. Ideally, the Church should have a strategy which is mission-led rather than resource-led. It should look at how many clergy it needs to meet its aspirations in serving the nation as a whole. It cannot, however, ignore the question of how to secure the resources to support them. The Church should also, for example, ensure that its discussions about the nature of the Church's current mission are taken into account when candidates are selected for ordination . . . Central and diocesan bodies often strive to do their best, sometimes taking on responsibilities which are not within their core functions, but gaps remain. There is no strategic overview.[13]

In addition to consensus based upon professional autonomy, a second assumption concerns the use of incremental budgeting. Incremental budgeting can be seen as the system of resource allocation in which allowances for inflation has been added year by year without any questions being asked about whether the final distribution actually accords with current priorities. Like consensus leadership, incremental budgeting seeks to be fair. Just as consensus leadership seeks to give an equal voice to majorities and minorities alike, so incremental budgeting seeks to give equal (even if diminishing) financial resources to all. In reality, both are strategies for inaction: both are deeply conservative. They often ensure that an organisation is unable to change and must accept, instead, its own gradual demise.

Again in *The Myth of the Empty Church*, I argue that incremental budgeting within churches does little to help them respond effectively to rapid changes in society. It has ensured that the Church of England and, to a lesser extent, the Methodist Church, has remained disproportionately rural long after most of the population moved to urban and suburban areas. In both denominations rural church buildings still out-number their urban and suburban counterparts. And both (but especially the Church of England) continue to subsidise rural clerical salaries. The Church of England has also continued to

---

[13] para. 3.10.

maintain many city-centre parishes (the city churches in London are an obvious and long-standing example), which have long since lost effective surrounding populations. Incremental budgeting, allowing an unquestioned use of subsidy, is largely responsible for this.

In contrast, we argue in *Strategic Church Leadership* that strategic planning would suggest that jobs and the budgets that support them always have to be justified – even when these budgets are apparently still in surplus. This is the essence of zero-based budgeting. Strategic planning builds a system of rigorous inspection into the process of deployment at every level. An appointment resulting from a vacancy has to be justified in terms of the aims of the organisation as a whole. It is not sufficient to argue that that particular post has always been filled in the past. It must still be needed and it should preferably have potential to be developed further in the future. Otherwise the resources might be deployed more effectively in some other area of the organisation.

## A Theological Re-appropriation

There is one further point that needs to be explored. The assumption behind the first part of this chapter has been that management theories can be treated as technique rather than ideology. The force of the second part has been that consensual/ autonomous and incremental styles of management are not quite as morally pure as many assume. However, in the final part I will explore another possibility – namely that some of the new management concepts, far from being secular notions imported inappropriately into churches, are in reality theological borrowings. If this is in fact the case, it could just be that a critical appropriation of new management concepts represents a fascinating instance of Weberian transposition and re-transposition. Theological notions having been borrowed and re-shaped by management theorists, are then re-appropriated by church leaders, albeit with sharper contours than they had before they were borrowed in the first place.

I doubt if he intended his work to be used for this purpose, but the recent writings of Stephen Pattison are highly instructive. Pattison is the author of three important works in pastoral theology: *A Critique of Pastoral Care*,[14] *Alive and Kicking*[15] and *Pastoral Care and Liberation Theology*.[16] After lecturing in the subject at Birmingham University, in the 1980s he retrained in management studies and is now a lecturer in the School of Health and Social Welfare of the Open University.

What he argues is that 'the new managers are deeply involved in religious activity . . . indeed in religious activity which has close analogies with charismatic evangelical Christianity' of which they are largely unaware.[17] Pointing to the immense changes in the British National Health Service resulting from the recommendations of Roy Griffiths in 1984, Pattison argues that quasi-religious language often accompanied these changes. He traces the roots of this language to the connection in the United States between the business and evangelical worlds. This language contains significant eschatological features as well as clear elements of 'faith'. In particular, the process of management by objectives is an area in which 'the vivid apocalyptic language of early Christianity has its greatest contemporary currency'. Having made this analysis, Pattison argues that managers need to learn to refine and scrutinise the metaphors that they use, just as critical theologians have learned over the years to do this with their language. Thus 'if people are involved in what is in many ways religious activity with important faith assumptions and a language of faith . . . they should be self-aware and self-critical'. In effect, 'managers should become much more openly and honestly theologians'.

It is not too difficult to see this process of transposition in some of the key concepts of new management theory. Terms such as 'mission statements', 'faith' and 'visions' are manifestly theological borrowings. Yet so might be such key concepts as 'accountability' and 'ownership' (for which read 'judgment'

[14] SCM Press, London, 1988.
[15] SCM Press, London, 1989.
[16] CUP, Cambridge, 1994.
[17] Stephen Pattison, 'Mystical Management: A Religious Critique of General Management in the Public Sector', *MC*, now entitled *Modern Believing*, XXXIII, 3, 1991, pp. 17–27.

and 'conversion'). Church leaders may well hesitate about endorsing such concepts merely on the grounds that they have been borrowed from Christianity. Some might also share Pattison's own suspicion of the specifically evangelical context of this borrowing. Nevertheless they might learn to be hesitant about depicting these concepts simply as 'secular'. Their theological roots might even modify Richard Roberts' analysis that Turnbull is yet another example whereby 'the episcopal elite in the Church of England has almost invariably tended to absorb and transmit the dominant ideology of its peer group'.[18]

Recently a number of management writers have made these theological connections explicit. Tom Chappell's *The Soul of a Business: Managing for Profit and the Common Good*[19] provides an unusual example of a successful business entrepreneur-turned-theologian. President and co-founder in the 1970s with his wife of Tom's of Maine – which produces natural toothpaste and related personal-care products – he enrolled in 1986 for a Master's degree at (the decidedly non-evangelical) Harvard Divinity School, in order 'to know more about how my life fitted into God's plan, what greater meaning my life's work had'.[20] Once enrolled, he was much impressed by the relationism of theologians such as Martin Buber and came to believe that it was possible to manage a business both for profit and for the common good. His whole book seeks to justify this belief.

Charles Handy provides a better-known but less elaborate example. Until recently his two persona – that of management guru and religious commentator/broadcaster – have usually been kept relatively separate. Towards the end of *The Empty Raincoat: Making Sense of the Future*[21] they explicitly merge. Having explored some of the paradoxes facing modern managers in a perplexing world, he writes:

> There is a haunting passage in the Book of Revelation in the Bible: 'to anyone who prevails, the Spirit says, I will give a white stone, on which is written a new name which no one

[18] Roberts, op. cit.
[19] Bantam, New York, 1993.
[20] p. xi.
[21] Arrow, London, 1995.

knows except he who receives it.' I keep a white stone on my desk as a reminder of my uniqueness. Even if there is no point, even if it is all a game of science, we must still believe that there is a point. If we don't believe that, there will be no reason to do anything, change anything. The world would be then at the mercy of all those who did believe that they could change things. It is a risk we cannot run.[22]

He argues that there are three senses which can foster this belief: a sense of continuity, a sense of connection, and a sense of direction. When articulating these increasingly teleological points he is careful to be inclusive. Using language reminiscent of Robert Bellah's understanding of civil religion[23] – language 'designed' to offend neither Christian nor Jew and neither transcendent nor immanent theist – he always depicts these three senses in highly inclusive and general terms.

The final chapter 'A Sense of Direction' illustrates this version of civil religion very clearly. Handy opens it with an account of Francis Fukuyama's *The End of History and the Last Man*.[24] He believes that it is essential for people to find 'a cause beyond themselves' if they are to overcome the comfort and boredom that Fukuyama depicts: 'if we are not machines, random accidents in the evolutionary chain, we need to have a sense of direction.'[25] Alongside theological references to St Augustine and to an anonymous Benedictine monk, he also includes more secular references to Maslow, Laura Ashley, Mayor Dinks and Tolstoy. All, he believes, point to the need for a cause which 'to be truly satisfying must be a purpose beyond oneself'.[26] At the same time he suggests that 'most of the religions have got it wrong':

> There may be some future existence after death, for all that we know, but it will certainly not be expressed in bodily shape, or in time or in space. It is, therefore, literally inconceivable, and, as a result, not something which I myself can take seriously.

[22] p. 239.
[23] Robert Bellah, *The Broken Covenant: American Civil Religion in Time of Trial,* Seabury Press, New York, 1975.
[24] Hamish Hamilton, London, 1992.
[25] p. 263.
[26] p. 264.

> My purpose in this life, as I read the teachings of the sages, is to so live that others can live better after I have gone, that, if I live on in any sense, I may live on in the continuing lives of others. Heaven and hell I see as medieval forms of social control, along with theories of reincarnation.[27]

He admits that it is difficult, in the conditions of comfortable democracy, to find a cause 'which lifts the efforts of the comfortable ones'. However, in the end, he believes simply that 'we have to fashion our own directions in our own places'.[28] Autonomy and pluralism are thus paradoxically combined with teleology. Direction and purpose are essential but, in a postmodern age, they are purposes and directions of our separate choosings.

Chappell shows a very similar combination. He offers six guidelines or 'permissions' for his employees: be clear, seek goodness, have faith, grasp autonomy, respect creation, and work together. Despite his own explicit Christianity, he too is careful to depict these guidelines in general and highly inclusive terms. So his depiction of 'seek goodness' is: 'Relationships with everyone inside and outside the company are central. There is more to business than the bottom line.' And that of 'have faith' is: 'Many of our challenges are too big for us alone. Have faith that others will help, and trust that life is about more than work. Faith is the source of patience and perseverance.'[29]

Such postmodern combinations of autonomy and pluralism with teleology are not without intellectual problems. Is any 'sense of direction' or 'faith' desirable? What about the faith and sense of direction of the serial killer or the fundamentalist bomber? Handy's, and even Chappell's, conclusions suffer from the weaknesses attached to the rhetoric of civil religion. Neither has the theological sophistication of Ian Markham's *Plurality and Christian Ethics*.[30] But that is not my point. However solipsistic, their conclusions offer a striking example of the interaction of theological and new management concepts. For a theologian the theology they offer, and especially that offered

[27] ibid.
[28] p. 267.
[29] p. 212.
[30] CUP, Cambridge, 1995.

by Handy, may well appear somewhat eviscerated. But that, too, is not my point. Rather my point is that Handy's widely read conclusions, together with those of less well known entrepreneurs such as Chappell, reinforce the suggestion that some of the new management concepts, far from being secular notions imported inappropriately into churches, are in reality theological borrowings. Instinctively Turnbull may have sensed this. Doubtless most church leaders will wish to reborrow these concepts carefully and critically. However they might think twice before adopting Richard Roberts' thoroughgoing hermeneutical suspicion. In the circumstances, a critical reappropriation of theologico-management concepts might seem more apt.

# IO

━┼🌑┼━

# *Euthanasia*

In my early collection *Christian Ethics in Secular Worlds* I included one item on 'AIDS and Social Policy' which was in the form of a briefing paper. I deliberately kept it in that format rather than changing it into essay format, both to preserve precision and to reflect the contribution of a variety of experts to its formation. It arose from an inter-professional group which met regularly at Newcastle. Since coming to Canterbury I have been involved in a number of similar working groups concerned with briefing church leaders. In this present collection I have decided to include two similar briefing papers – this one on the vexed question of euthanasia and the next on the highly complex issues arising from the possibilities of gene therapies. In both papers I have consulted widely and received very expert advice, but finally I take full responsibility for their contents. These are emphatically not consensus reports from working groups which other members have to own in public.

The first briefing paper arose as a response to two tragic cases of 'euthanasia' which have been widely discussed in the media since 1992. The Dr Cox case involved a physician who gave a terminally ill woman (on her request) life-shortening but non-palliative medication. She died soon afterwards, but his actions were reported by one of the nurses involved and he was prosecuted for murder. In the end he was reprimanded for his action, but found not guilty of murder on the narrow grounds that, since the woman was cremated, it was impossible to determine whether she had died from the medication or from her illness. The Tony Bland case involved a teenager who was crushed and deprived of oxygen in the Hillsborough football disaster. He remained in a comatose state, with no evident cortical activity (and thus without any cognition or sensation) for the next three-and-a-half years. Since his reflexes were still intact he was able to breathe spontaneously, but otherwise he required intensive nursing in order to survive. His case came to the courts because his family repeatedly requested that he should be allowed to die. In contrast to the Cox case, the medical authorities in the Bland case were not prepared to comply without the agreement of the courts (even though compliance here involved only the withdrawal, not the giving of 'treatment').

The second briefing paper – or more accurately collection of three briefing papers – is concerned with medical developments in the areas of genetic screening and therapy. These fast-developing areas are raising a series of fascinating but complex moral issues. In exploring them the work of the Nuffield Council on Bioethics has been invaluable. In the last three years working parties of the Council have to date produced three excellent reports on *Genetic Screening, Human Tissues* and *Xenografts*.[1] Each is a model of how meaningful ethical discussions can still be made across disciplinary, ideological and religious divides even in a postmodern age. This is no small achievement: postmodernity and scientific and technological developments in areas such as genetics do not make easy bedfellows. As William Schweiker argues convincingly,[2] there is an urgent need for ethical responsibility within an age that has an awkward combination of increasing pluralism and technological power. As power increases in the world today – not just in the political and military orders but also in such areas as genetics and biotechnology – so ironically does pluralism. The latter ensures that people become increasingly confused about the bases of public morality just at the very moment that they are possessing an unprecedented amount of power. Schweiker believes that a combination of corporate and individual responsibility is

[1] Nuffield Council on Bioethics, Bedford Square, London.
[2] William Schweiker, *Responsibility and Christian Ethics*, CUP, Cambridge and New York, 1995.

urgently required and that churches have a significant contribution to make to both.

If church leaders are indeed to contribute meaningfully to the public discussion of these two sets of moral issues, then they clearly do need to be adequately briefed. Hence the origin of these two briefing papers. Nevertheless, I am very conscious that in both areas details are changing very fast. I fear that they will have changed even in the time that it takes to publish them now. Christian ethics remains a risky business.

### *Euthanasia*

1.1 This briefing paper intends to do three things: firstly to pinpoint some of the key changes in perception that have recently taken place in relation to the broad issue of euthanasia; secondly to reflect some recent theological discussion in this area; and thirdly to suggest ethical and theological positions that might be adopted by church leaders as the issue of euthanasia is raised in public.

1.2 The Cox and Bland cases have recently raised public consciousness about 'euthanasia' in Britain – although it is also a topic that is being widely discussed elsewhere in Europe and in the United States. There is likely to be continuing political pressure and growing public support for various forms of euthanasia to be the subject of permissive legislation. In very broad terms, the Cox case has highlighted the issue of medically assisted death, the Bland case that of medically prolonged permanently unconscious life, and both have pointed to a third issue relating to patient autonomy and Living Wills. All three are issues which will, I believe, continue to require periodic responses from church leaders.

1.3 Euthanasia as such is an impossibly wide topic – ranging from (*a*) withholding or withdrawing treatment from a mature, rational, conscious, terminally ill patient refusing life-prolonging treatment, through to (*z*) active, direct termination of a permanently comatose or mentally incapacitated patient's life. Given this wide range very few people can be wholly for or even wholly against every form of euthanasia. For example, it

would be illegal for a pro-life doctor to treat a patient, contrary
to her rationally expressed wishes, in situation (*a*), and very
few advocates of 'direct' or 'active' euthanasia recommend that
*all* permanently comatose or mentally incapacitated patients'
lives in situation (*z*) should be actively terminated. Unlike
debates about abortion, ethical debates about euthanasia are
almost always about degrees rather than about absolutes. So,
whereas the abortion debate has often become polarised
between pro-life and pro-choice absolutist positions, debates
about euthanasia are characteristically about 'crossing lines' or
about 'slippery slopes'.

1.4 Medical developments make ethical questions about
euthanasia (and many other issues in medical ethics) increasingly complex. For example, the Bland case was made possible
by forms of intensive nursing care and the use of antibiotics
which would not have been possible earlier in the century. As
medicine develops it becomes possible to keep alive for much
longer many with severe disabilities (possibly for twenty years
for young people like Tony Bland). Whilst this might often be
thought to be highly desirable, it also makes possible some
highly distressing cases. Furthermore, as medicine becomes
increasingly sophisticated, so it inevitably raises public expectations. For example, in the Cox case it was apparently assumed
by some that doctors should be able to eliminate pain. Since in
this respect Dr Cox 'failed', he should be allowed (it was
assumed ) to terminate the life of the patient as she herself
requested.

*Changing Perceptions*

2.1 The British Medical Association remains opposed to 'active'
or 'direct' forms of euthanasia; however there has been a distinct
shift between its *Euthanasia Report* of 1988 and its September
1992 *Discussion Paper on Treatment of Patients in Persistent
Vegetative State*. In the second it held that 'artificial feeding is
a medical treatment and that medical treatment can be
withdrawn on the basis of a clinical decision'. The BMA
medical ethics committee argued specifically that 'feeding by

gastrostomy or nasogastric tube is an artificial process akin to ventilation'. The BMA guidelines in 1993 specified that this process should not be withdrawn unless a persistent vegetative state (PVS) patient had been in that state for at least a year and two independent doctors and the doctor caring for the patient believed that there was no reasonable chance of improvement.

2.2 The Institute of Medical Ethics adopted a similar position on PVS patients, but went further than the BMA on 'active' or 'direct' forms of euthanasia. A majority of the IME's 1990 working party held that: 'the doctor, acting in good conscience, is ethically justified in assisting death if the need to relieve intense and unceasing pain or distress caused by an incurable illness greatly outweighs the benefit to the patient of further prolonging his life.' They insisted, however, that it is important that the 'sustained wishes' of the patient on this issue should be known to the doctor.

2.3 The distinguished Appleton International Conference Project, begun in 1987, reported its *Developing Guidelines for Decisions to Forgo Life-Prolonging Medical Treatment* in September 1992. In two respects, again by a majority decision, it went considerably beyond the BMA position. On PVS patients it argued that: 'The patient who is reliably diagnosed as being in a PVS has no self-regarding interests. Consequently, unless a previously expressed advance directive requests it, there is no patient-based reason to continue life-sustaining treatments, including artificial hydration and nutrition. It is unkind to allow unrealistic optimism to be sustained and it is unfair to allow the prolonged consumption of societal resources in support of such patients beyond a period of education and adjustment for the family.' In other works, the authors of the report believed that patients' prior wishes (e.g. Living Will) should be required to opt in to 'artificial' hydration/nutrition, not to opt out of it. And secondly, it argued that: 'Patients having decision-making capacity who are severely and irremediably suffering from incurable diseases sometimes ask for assistance in dying. Such requests for active termination of life by a medical act which directly and intentionally causes death may be morally justifiable and should be given serious consideration.'

2.4 Following the Cox trial of September 1992, both *The Independent* and *The Times* in their leaders expressed sympathy for Cox, but finally argued against a change in legislation. However, the editor of the *British Medical Journal* called for a Royal Commission on the issue. Instructively he argued that: 'More perhaps than any other, Britain is a post-religious society, where theological notions like the sanctity of life should not be overvalued . . . More and more doctors do seem to consider euthanasia acceptable in strictly defined circumstances.' And the editorial of *The Lancet* argued that: the BMA should 'look again across the North Sea [i.e. to Holland] and abandon the unsympathetic public line to which we have been exposed in the past few days'.

2.5 The *House of Lords Judgment* of 3 February 1993, which finally allowed Tony Bland to die, offered a number of clarifications. The Appeal Judges agreed that the regime allowing Tony Bland to survive did constitute 'medical treatment and care', arguing that the function of artificial feeding by naso-gastric tube (let alone of evacuating through enemas and catheters) 'is to provide a form of life support analogous to that provided by a ventilator which artificially breathes air in and out of the lungs of a patient incapable of breathing normally, thereby enabling oxygen to reach the bloodstream'. A consequence of this analogy is that 'if in either case the treatment is futile . . . it can properly be concluded that it is no longer in the best interests of the patient to continue it'. There was also general agreement that the notion of 'best interests of the patient' should only be applied to him positively rather than negatively – i.e. it could not accurately be claimed that, since he lacked cognition or sensation, it was in Tony Bland's best interests for his life to be terminated, but it was finally deemed to be in his best interests not to continue invasive medical treatment/care indefinitely and to no purpose. The Judges mentioned deep misgivings about the case and several called for a review of the law and ethics in this area. A concern was also expressed about a need to consider the best interests of the community at large raised by this specific case.

2.6 Following this judgment, and Tony Bland's subsequent death, a select committee was, as requested by the Appeal Judges, set up in the House of Lords to consider the ethical issues involved. This committee's *Report on Medical Ethics* was published in January 1994. It considered at length the issue of direct, active euthanasia, finally rejecting the possibility of legislation to allow this in Britain. The committee also considered PVS at length, but crucially failed to reach agreement on whether or not nutrition/hydration in this context constituted medical treatment (representatives of the nursing profession were reluctant to agree that it was). As a result the committee proposed no legislation for PVS cases, but called instead for professional guidelines. Each request for withdrawal of hydration/ventilation must therefore still come to Court (in Scotland the first case came to Court on a similar basis, but four years later, in 1996).

2.7 In March 1996 the Royal College of Physicians issued guidelines recommending the use of the term 'permanent vegetative state' (rather than persistent) where irreversibility can be diagnosed with a high degree of certainty. According to these guidelines no diagnosis should be made before twelve months after a head injury or six months after brain damage from other causes. The diagnosis should then be made by two doctors experienced in assessing disturbances of consciousness, whose main role is to ensure that the patient is not sentient. In reaching a diagnosis they should listen carefully to relatives, carers and nursing staff responsible for the patient.

2.8 Unfortunately the RCP guidelines were issued just a week before Dr Keith Andrews of the Royal Hospital for Neuro-disability in Putney reported two diagnosed PVS patients (one in a coma for seven years) who had apparently managed to communicate with hospital staff. These cases may suggest either that PVS diagnosis has not always been very reliable in the past or that a 'persistent' state can never be deemed with certainty to be a 'permanent' state. However the Scottish judge did examine evidence about these two cases before deciding still to allow withdrawal in 1996.

### Ethical Considerations

3.1 In recent Christian ethical discussion in this area there has been controversy about whether or not PVS patients could still be considered to be 'persons' or full human beings. So the *House of Lords Judgment* graphically described how Tony Bland's cerebral cortex 'has resolved into a watery mass. The cortex is that part of the brain which is the seat of cognitive function and sensory capacity. Anthony Bland cannot see, hear or feel anything. He cannot communicate in any way. The consciousness which is the essential feature of individual personality has departed for ever'. If PVS patients are not 'persons' then, presumably, actively terminating their lives presents far fewer ethical problems than if they are persons. An animal, for example, could simply be 'put down'. A corpse could simply be put into a box.

3.2 Manifestly PVS patients fall into neither of these categories. They are not 'brain dead' in any modern, technical sense. Again *The House of Lords Judgment* argues that 'the brain stem, which controls the reflexive functions of the body, in particular heartbeat, breathing and digestion, continues to operate. In the eyes of the medical world and of the law a person is not clinically dead so long as the brain stem retains its function'. Such patients do still require to be accorded respect as 'persons', albeit as persons no longer capable of interpersonal, let alone spiritual, relationships. At the very least they still possess a continuing personal history and should be respected for who they once were. Just as society should respect the senile, so they should respect PVS patients.

3.3 A decision to withhold or withdraw 'treatment' (accepting that the nutrition/hydration/evacuation regime of PVS patients is indeed treatment) is thus a decision not to treat a 'person' considered now, according to the best available means of diagnosis, to be permanently incapable of actively initiating, let alone of sustaining, *any* personal relationships whatsoever. Actively terminating the lives of such patients would have very damaging implications for other groups of vulnerable people in society – especially the senile and those with very severe mental disabilities. Yet treating them indefinitely, invasively and to no obvious personal benefit (unless the faint possibility of some reversal is considered to be such a benefit), also seems morally unacceptable.

3.4 There may be little formal difference between withholding and withdrawing treatment. However, there is an important moral difference. Those who withdraw treatment have at least attempted to do something, albeit something which is now recognised as hopeless. It would be wrong if they were to be at greater risk of moral blame than those who simply withheld treatment at the outset (although ironically they are at present far more vulnerable in terms of the law).

3.5 Families need to be given time to realise that such a person is permanently comatose: families of the vulnerable do need to be protected. Nonetheless families often have a false hope that a PVS condition might be significantly reversed (even after twelve months) or that one day there will be some dramatic new 'cure'.

3.6 Decisions about withdrawing or not withdrawing 'treatment' from such patients do raise important questions about how society uses finite health care resources. Nonetheless, such cases should not be resolved solely on the basis of materialist criteria. Indeed, there is always a danger that cost-cutting authorities or governments might be tempted to regard PVS patients as an obvious saving. This is a vulnerable group and individuals within it need especial protection until medical authorities are convinced that their condition is irreversible. The cases of apparent reverse cited by Dr Andrews and others do need to be inspected very carefully – a safe diagnosis of PVS is essential to an ethical decision to withdraw.

## Ethical Recommendations

4.1 I believe that it is crucial for church leaders to show a mixture of pastoral concern and wise caution in this area. Euthanasia in its various forms involves people at their most vulnerable. The dangers of a culture that marginalises any theologically based considerations are real (*vide* the *BMJ* editorial), but so are the fears that most of us have, whether we are theologically committed or not, that one day we ourselves will be suspended between life and death. However protective we are of others in such a condition, few of us wish this to happen to ourselves. Indeed few of us may wish this to happen to ourselves even if there is a very slim chance that in some very few cases some reversal might be possible.

4.2 Euthanasia involves a very different cluster of ethical issues from abortion, but the politics of the two have a certain affinity. On the issue of abortion (and on divorce) in the 1960s the Church of England's Board of Social Responsibility supported changes in law, but discovered later that the actual changes *de facto* were far more permissive than it had intended. Whatever is now thought about the Abortion Act, any ecclesiastical support for permissive legislation (or permissive agreements as in Holland) on euthanasia will need to be far more astute at a political level.

4.3 Choosing between the two dominant metaphors in the current euthanasia debate, that of 'crossing the line' might be preferred to that of the 'slippery slope'. Skiers are well aware that slippery slopes are desirable and negotiable challenges. More seriously, to object to something simply because it might give rise to something else is an objection to the 'something else' and not to the original 'something'. It simply means that one has to be very careful to preclude the 'something else'. Thus, agreeing to EXIT's proposals is not in itself to be committed to Hitler's final solutions (Hitler regularly appears in slippery slope arguments!). Once aware of possible abuses one should be able to guard against them more effectively.

4.4 'Crossing the line' suggests instead that, however traumatic the particular cases, allowing or encouraging doctors actively to take life puts them into a new and possibly damaged relationship with their other patients. (The *House of Lords Judgment* noticeably avoided 'slippery slope arguments' – being concerned instead with the 'line' between legality and illegality.) It is important to stress that the interests of the patient, the family and society at large are all involved in 'crossing lines'.

4.5 Another social metaphor (but drawn from the business rather than military worlds) might be 'changing the culture': instead of 'caring culture' doctors could be changing to a mechanistic or purely functional culture. I suspect that it is this which the BMA most fears. Since the church can, at least in part, claim to be the mother of the caring professions, it is appropriate that it should support this BMA position.

4.6 One of the advantages of using a more social metaphor is to draw attention to the limitations of the increasing use in medical ethics of the concept of 'autonomy'. Most might agree that patient autonomy *is* important – most of us in the West value freedom and are suspicious of the 'State' attempting to run our private lives. Yet the concept of autonomy when used in isolation is ethically limited. It can easily lead to a demand-led rather than needs-led health service and in the process the inarticulate and vulnerable can be overlooked. Those who demand most in the name of personal autonomy are not necessarily the most needy, and vice versa. In the euthanasia debate, patient demands are important but are not the only factor that should be considered.

4.7 From this it might be appropriate that Living Wills should only be seen as morally binding for withholding/withdrawing treatment and not for assisted death. They could become relevant to a decision, for example, about whether or not to continue invasive treatment on a PVS patient. But it would be very damaging to society at large and to doctor–patient relationships if they ever became directly related to medically assisted death.

4.8 All of this suggests that church leaders might:

> (*a*) support the *House of Lords Judgement* on Bland and support BMA and RCP guidelines about how prolonged treatment on other PVS patients can, with adequate safeguards and vigilant inspection of cases of apparent reversal, be withdrawn without recourse on each occasion to the Courts.

(*b*) oppose any attempt to legalise medically assisted death and to insist that this issue should not be conflated with (*a*);

(*c*) offer caution about Living Wills if they discuss medically assisted death, but support them if they do not.

## A Theological Basis

5.1 It is 'care' (in the form of *agape*), not the automatic relief of pain *per se*, which is central to pastoral theology in this area. For the Christian, Christ is seen to identify with our sufferings but not always to relieve us of suffering. In Christ we believe we can see meaning and value beyond our sufferings, even if we cannot always see meaning and value within these sufferings. This is not to welcome pain and suffering, but it is to be guided by the belief that their instant relief is not in itself the highest good.

5.2 If indefinite nutrition / hydration by nasogastric or gastrostomy tube and evacuation by catheters and enemas on a permanently comatose patient does seem to be medical treatment designed to prolong life, then care / *agape* might eventually involve withdrawing it. For the Christian this is not the only life and there is no requirement to prolong it needlessly. Life perceived as God-given is always to be treated with respect, with gratitude, and with responsibility, but it is not in itself 'sacred' (a Hindu more than a Christian concept). Whilst such a perception might make most Christians cautious about sanctioning the deliberate taking of life, it might also discourage them from clinging pointlessly to it.

# II

⚬⊷✺⊶⚬

# Gene Therapies

## A Preliminary Map

### 1. The Genome Project

The international attempt to map the human genome has raised a number of ethical dilemmas. Amongst them are the following:

1.1 Who 'owns' the information generated by this project? Those who believe that it is right to patent the information argue that this prevents secrecy (since all those who want to have the information can pay for it) and rewards research. Those opposed argue that it is inappropriate to patent data already present in the natural order and introduces commercial greed into science.

1.2 Genetic information from the project is obviously vital to long-term genetic therapy, but it is also vulnerable to social and political abuse. There are fears of returning to Nazi eugenic abuses or moving into the data information abuses parallel to those being raised currently by public computer networks.

1.3 As an aid to genetic therapy there is also some doubt about whether the benefits will outweigh the disadvantages. The potential benefits to those who might be 'cured' from serious genetic disorders are obvious. But others with serious genetic disorders, which cannot be 'cured', may be considerably disadvantaged (in terms of employment, insurance and even peace of mind) by a knowledge of their genetic future acquired through screening.

## 2. Individual Gene Therapy

Clinical trials in the USA and Europe have already begun using a variety of techniques involving gene-transfer experiments – with the aim of replacing defective genes with healthy substitutes. Potentially there could be therapeutic benefit to patients with malignant tumours, cystic fibrosis, and many other inherited disorders caused by single defective genes. In February 1993 permission was given in Britain for the first gene-transfer experiment – an attempt to benefit children with adenosine deaminase (ADA) deficiency. Because such therapy is still experimental and potentially far-reaching, it raises a series of moral dilemmas:

2.1 Whilst knowledge of the human genome is still developing, can the potential risks be adequately measured? There may be risks not just to the patients (who initially may have otherwise terminal genetic defects), but also to the medical teams, to the families and contacts, and possibly to future generations (if the changes effected enter the germ line). The use, for example, of viral vectors may carry dangers of affecting others or of affecting patients themselves in unplanned and damaging ways.

2.2 As more and more people with genetic defects are enabled to live and reproduce, so the human genetic pool may contain an increasing amount of various defects. If this happens, the long-term deterioration of human genes might be another example of modern medicine producing new problems when it resolves existing problems (iatrogenesis).

2.3 Linked to this are questions about the ethics of resource allocation. How much should society spend upon developing genetic therapy rather than upon more conventional forms of medicine?

2.4 Genetic release into the environment is already causing moral concern – for example, the effect upon the environment, the effects on the food chain, the depletion of genetic variety, the over-dependency upon international conglomerates producing genetically improved grain and so forth. Once genetic therapy becomes widespread, will it not add to fears about 'improving' the natural order?

2.5 How far should animals be used in the interests of gene therapy? There are likely to be increasing uses of human genetic material in animals, for example to allow organ transplants from animals into humans (xenografts). At what point does this become unethical?

### 3. Germ Line Therapy

As yet germ line therapy – the attempt to alter the genetic inheritance of humans before or immediately after fertilisation – is a prospect for the future (although it is already taking place in the agricultural world). However, it raises some of the most acute moral dilemmas:

3.1 The potential risks are far greater than 2.1. It is possible that by changing the single cell 'defects' of an individual there may be unforeseen effects upon future generations. Even when a full map of the human genome is produced, the effects of altering genetic inheritance will still be largely unknown. Future generations may be severely disadvantaged by our experiments now (cf. current fears about the effects of twentieth-century technology upon the environment).

3.2 Much of medicine takes risks in the early stages, but hitherto these risks have not involved future generations directly. Does the prospect of germ line therapy represent a qualitative change in medicine?

3.3 Even if the dilemmas raised in 2.2 are reduced with the prospect of germ line therapy, those in 2.3 and 2.4 are considerably heightened.

3.4 The future prospects of biotechnology raise the overall issue of whether what could be done should be done. But the issue is complicated by the cynic's observation that what can be done surely will be done by someone, somewhere, sometime.

### Genetic Screening

4.1 This map raises a wide variety of ethical issues, but of these two may be of particular importance for church leaders. The initial report of the Nuffield Council on Bioethics focused upon

**genetic screening** since this is already being developed and is likely soon to become more widespread. However, in a context of extraordinary developments in animal biotechnology, the possible implications of **modifying human origins** is also an issue which it would be wise for church leaders also to consider now.

4.2 In examining the ethical issues surrounding genetic screening, the Nuffield Report is aware that it is entering an area which is still developing. Commendably this is a report which for once attempts to anticipate ethical issues. The issues anticipated in its initial brief were:

- (*a*)  the general risk of stigma attaching or being attached to those perceived as genetically disadvantaged;
- (*b*)  the handling and holding of information;
- (*c*)  consent to being screened;
- (*d*)  confidentiality in all its aspects;
- (*e*)  the implications for employment and insurance;
- (*f*)  the storage and use of genetic information for legal purposes.

I will focus here upon (*c*), (*d*) and (*e*).

## Consent and Counselling

5.1 The Nuffield Report argues that properly informed patient consent in genetic screening requires a mixture of intelligible literature and active counselling. Literature alone would be insufficient if patients are adequately to understand the aims and implications of genetic screening. Truly informed consent and provision for counselling are thus linked.

5.2 Truly informed consent implies that those to be screened are made aware of any substantial risks, are given adequate time to decide whether or not to allow the screening, and are free to withdraw from the screening at any point. None of this is easy in the context of a busy primary care surgery.

5.3 The unusual features of genetic screening, as distinct from other forms of screening, are that: (*a*) genetic screening may have direct implications, especially when single gene defects are detected, for other members of the patient's family; (*b*) there is at present little that can be done to remedy defective genes;

(*c*) the health implications of many defective genes (with the exception of single gene defects) are at present only partially understood. As a result of genetic screening, patients may thus be given information about their genetic inheritance, which they can do little or nothing about, whose health implications are often unclear, but which are likely to involve other members of their family.

5.4 Despite these features, the Nuffield Report concludes that truly informed consent is possible, provided that adequate counselling is available at all stages of the screening process: 'This will require the diffusion of an understanding of genetics (at present mainly confined to genetic counsellors) in particular among those engaged in primary care.'

5.5 Given the current pressures on primary care, is there a possibility of counselling in a non-clinical environment? In such a highly technical area there is an obvious need for adequate training and accurate, up-to-date information. It is unlikely that church groups could be expected to meet such counselling needs. However, there might well be an important role for self-help voluntary groups ( in which church members are often prominent members). Other areas of disability suggest that strongly motivated individuals in self-help groups can acquire the necessary skills and expertise.

5.6 At an ethical and theological level it might still be important for church leaders to offer some caution in this area. Enthusiasm for new knowledge can sometimes outweigh the needs of the vulnerable. The Christian Gospel always gives priority to the vulnerable and needy in a way that secular society sometimes forgets. For example, even the possibility of genetic defects (however unclear their implications) may place some women under strong social pressure to have an abortion. Viewed in a wider context, genetic 'defects' might sometimes be regarded instead as genetic 'opportunities'. The very flexibility of our genetic inheritance may be an essential part of creation.

5.7 Nevertheless, the importance of genetic screening for certain single gene defects cannot properly be ignored. The deep distress that the diseases that can be caused by them bring to many families means that it is right for medicine to proceed in this area – albeit with sensitivity and proper caution.

*Confidentiality*

6.1 The unusual features of genetic screening (5.3) raise complex ethical issues in relation to confidentiality. The normal expectation of the individual patient for medical confidentiality is problematic precisely because genetic screening may reveal *familial* genetic defects. On the other hand, the untreatable and partially understood nature of many genetic defects might militate against breaching patient confidentiality. Thus, the individual may be unwilling to disclose information about an *inherited* and *inheritable* genetic defect to other members of his or her family. At the same time that individual might argue that there is little certain benefit at present from disclosure.

6.2 The Nuffield Report argues, on grounds of both principle and prudence, that confidentiality should normally be respected in genetic screening. Increasing patient autonomy and professional standards based upon trust both require that confidentiality should be the norm. The future co-operation of the public in programmes of genetic screening also makes a policy of confidentiality prudent.

6.3 Yet the Report argues that, in the area of genetic screening, the duty of confidentiality is not absolute. When an individual refuses to disclose genetic information to other relatives which could be to their benefit – even after extensive attempts at persuasion by the medical staff involved – then it might be right to breach confidentiality. In this instance, the interests of family members would override any rights of the individual to privacy – responsibility to others would take precedence over individual autonomy.

6.4 From this the Report concludes that: (i) confidentiality should be the norm in genetic screening; (ii) persuasion should be attempted when individuals are unwilling to disclose significant information to other family members; (iii) on those exceptional occasions when persuasion is ineffective, health professionals may sometimes rightly breach patient confidentiality.

6.5 There is some concern about whether the Nuffield Report has delineated sufficiently the proper circumstances for breaching patient confidentiality. Since the Report maintains that such decisions can only be made case by case, the risks of abuse (however rare) are obvious. Hard cases may indeed make bad laws.

6.6 Here too, since so many genetic defects are at present untreatable and only partially understood, there is a danger of individual coercion which may actually achieve very little. The Report argues for breaching confidentiality in relation to 'information arising from genetic screening that may be vital to the well-being or future well-being of other family members'. The phrase 'may be vital' in this sentence suggests some caution about breaching confidentiality. Who determines what is 'vital'? How strong does the 'may' have to be for confidentiality to be broken? And, in any case, can the doctor be sure that other members of the family actually wish to be informed? Caution is needed here.

*Insurance and Employment*

7.1 The ethical issues arising from insurance companies or employers discovering about the possible genetic defects of an individual are not new. The possibility of widespread genetic screening merely makes these issues more prevalent. Genetic screening makes an existing problem more acute.

7.2 The Nuffield Report is conscious that there is a very real possibility of abuses arising from the increasing availability of genetic screening. Insurance companies could require individuals to have genetic tests before offering them insurance. Many people might be disadvantaged by this, since insurance companies may tend to be over-cautious even about those genetic defects whose effects are largely unknown (indeed some genes which insurance companies in the West might regard as 'defects', such as the sickle cell gene, may actually be advantageous in different environments). Only a small number of people with a known family history of single gene defect, who then test negative themselves, would benefit from such required genetic screening.

7.3 The Report, therefore, recommends that 'British insurance companies should adhere to their current policy of not requiring any genetic tests as a prerequisite of obtaining insurance'. They also call for a temporary moratorium on requiring the disclosure of genetic data – unless individuals already have a known family history of genetic disease that can be established by conventional means or are seeking a large policy. This temporary moratorium should be used for early discussion between the Government and the insurance industry (a discussion now started with the House of Commons Select Committee Report on Genetic Screening).

7.4 The Nuffield Report expresses the fear that genetic screening may be used as a means to disadvantage people (for insurance or employment) who merely have a genetic predisposition to some disease. If insurance premiums were increased or jobs debarred, for those who tested positive, then many people would be discouraged from having genetic screening at all. A potential to future health and well-being (if that is what such screening really makes possible) would be hampered by fears relating to insurance (including much house-buying) and employment.

7.5 However, it can be assumed that insurance companies, even if they accept a temporary moratorium, are unlikely to ignore genetic data in the general population for long (they already use it for known genetically inherited disease). Once genetic information is known to individuals, under present law companies will surely require it to be disclosed if policies are not to be invalidated. This could well act as a major disincentive to genetic screening. As a result of such screening, individuals may make discoveries about their genes, which they are powerless to change, which they barely understand, but which still disadvantage them in terms of insurance and house-buying.

7.6 Again a concern for the vulnerable and disadvantaged is a crucial theological consideration. It is not simply the wealthy who rely upon insurance. Housing, pensions and parts of health-care are increasingly being covered by insurance. If the disclosure of genetic data also enters employment, then the vulnerable will be disadvantaged several times over. An aid to better health care will ironically have become another means of discrimination against the vulnerable. To put this another way, genetic discrimination will join other forms of racial, sexual and religious discrimination in society.

7.7 At best genetic screening seeks to help those who are at considerable risk from single gene defects. However, these considerations do suggest that caution and adequate safeguards are needed if a means to health is not instead to become a means of disadvantage and even discrimination.

7.8 Given these moral objections, it is desirable that the genetic information required by insurance companies about most people should be limited (if necessary by law) to family histories. Only those with established family risks – and for whom there might be an advantage, if proved negative, to be gained from genetic screening – could then legally be asked about data based upon this screening.

7.9 However, it must be a real sign of hope that the Nuffield Council on Bioethics could produce such an excellent report. It is to the credit of the members of the Council that it has succeeded in producing such a carefully balanced discussion of an ethical issue, largely *before it becomes a reality*. Its balance of caution and encouragement, of autonomy and responsibility, can be welcomed by church leaders.

## Modifying Human Origins

8.1 If genetic screening is one important issue for church leaders, a second is this: a generalised fear about modifying human origins surrounds the current debates about the newer forms of human fertility treatment and the emerging possibilities of germ line surgery. I will attempt now to identify some of the features of this fear and to suggest responses that it might be appropriate for church leaders to make.

8.2 The generalised fear can be stated quite simply. Many people react intuitively with a sense of horror at reports, for example, about post-menopausal women being enabled to become pregnant, or about the future possibilities of human cloning or gene modification. They often use language about humans 'playing God' or about 'fabricating human beings'. They imagine that the scientist will increasingly replace the father, or even the mother, in producing babies . . . along the lines of Aldous Huxley's famous parody *Brave New World.* And they fear that children will forfeit their sense of personal identity and that parenting (a new functional verb) will become too mechanical.

8.3 This generalised fear is often held paradoxically alongside a deep concern to help potential parents who are seriously disadvantaged. Perhaps it is a concern for childless couples who are desperate to have children of their own, and yet who find that even adoption is increasingly rare in a world which no longer stigmatises single parents. Or perhaps it is a concern to eliminate the more egregious single gene diseases – knowing that genetic counselling/screening is never fully effective since a desire to have babies can often overcome even known serious familial risks.

8.4 The combination of a fear of the social consequences of a particular development with a desire to help the seriously disadvantaged creates this paradox. There are obvious parallels to this in the current euthanasia debate which has just been examined. The campaign for legalised euthanasia is driven, not simply by a belief in patient autonomy, but also by a deep compassion for those reporting intractable pain and for the senile who have lost self-dignity. Yet the fear of the social, legal and medical consequences that might arise from legalised euthanasia conflicts with this deep compassion. Such fear has led most church leaders in Britain to oppose a change in the law or medical practice in relation to euthanasia, despite what appears to be strong popular support for it. Should a fear over the consequences of the newer forms of human fertility treatment and the possibility of human germ line surgery prompt a similar reaction by the church leaders?

## *A Generation Ago*

9.1 The Christian ethicist Paul Ramsey would undoubtedly have answered 'yes' to this question. His *Fabricated Man* (Yale University Press, New Haven, 1970) might be helpful in the present debate. Precisely because it was written a quarter-of-a-century ago, it is now possible to check the accuracy of some its predictions. Ramsey was concerned both with conventional fertility treatment (in his day AIH and AID, although he could foresee the possibility of the live births resulting from IVF which did become a reality in 1978) and with the still futuristic possibilities of biotechnology being used on embryos. He expressed two overall ethical objections – the first based upon the empirical consequences of new fertility techniques and the second based upon the humanistic and theological consequences of these techniques.

9.2 One empirical consequence concerned a possible increase in genetic deficiency resulting from these techniques: 'The fact is that because of our technical and medical competence and our proper concern for persons now alive, we are enabling people to reach the age of reproduction, and to reproduce when they do, in greater numbers than would have been the case in former ages' (p. 3). He used diabetics as an instructive example: 'After a cure was found in insulin, they were enabled to survive and lead useful lives. Since, however, they were not generally able to have children, these individuals were as genetically dead as if they had been stillborn. Now the safe delivery of the children of diabetic mothers is commonplace in all our hospitals; and as a consequence the incidence of diabetes in the population is irreversibly increasing' (pp. 3–4). Ramsey argued that the logic of this process, once applied to other conditions, entails that human genetic inheritance, if unchecked, might become increasingly defective – in other words, the human 'gene pool' might gradually deteriorate.

9.3 This leads naturally to a second empirical consequence. An obvious way out of the dilemma of a deteriorating genetic inheritance might one day be germ line treatment or 'genetic surgery'. Ramsey supported this idea in principle: 'Morally, genetic medicine enabling a man and a woman to engender a child without some defective gene they carry would seem to be as permissible as treatment to cure infertility when one of the partners bears this defect' (p. 44). However, in practice he advised caution because of the considerable risks involved. So he maintained that 'the complexity of our genetic mechanism in general might mean that it is unlikely that we will ever know enough assuredly to control remedial medical applications of genetic surgery – when this surgery is submitted to the test of 'a reasonable and well-examined expectation of doing more good than harm' to the patient to be born' (pp. 100–1). Indeed, he maintained that the enormous risks involved in the first experimental trials in genetic surgery meant that they could never be morally justified. He even argued (wrongly as we now know) that IVF techniques involved unacceptable physical risks to the babies that resulted from them.

9.4 At a more theological level he argued that new fertility treatments and genetics tend to distort God's creation: 'To put radically asunder what God joined together in parenthood when He made love procreative, to procreate from beyond the sphere of love (AID, for example, or making human life in a test-tube), or to posit acts of sexual love beyond the sphere of responsible procreation (by definition, marriage), means a refusal of the image of God's creation in our own. A science-based culture, such as the present one, of necessity erodes and makes nonsense out of all sorts of bonds and connections which a Christian sees to be the case' (p. 39).

9.5 Secondly, he argued that such treatments involve humans in 'questionable aspirations to Godhead'. He expressed this in terms of an aphorism: 'Men ought not to play God before they learn to be men, and after they have learned to be men they will not play God' (p. 138). He frankly doubted whether humans would ever have sufficient wisdom (moral or empirical) to use new fertility and genetic techniques responsibly and, as a result, was highly suspicious of humans attempting to 'play God'. In a very real sense, Ramsey argued, molecular biologists now move 'in a world where formerly only God abounded' (p. 146).

## The Arguments Today

10.1 What is to be made of these arguments today? Should they be taken seriously by ethicists and theologians?

10.2 The fact that Ramsey has been proved wrong about the physical dangers to babies produced by IVF might suggest that some of the dangers he foresaw in 9.3 can be exaggerated. In reality IVF techniques were well tested on farm animals long before they were first used on human beings. The birth of Louise Brown was preceded by the birth following IVF of many healthy cattle. On a similar basis it might be argued that long before germ line treatment is used on human beings its physical consequences will be well established in the agricultural world – as is indeed happening, first on new commercially produced food and next on farm animals. In this way the risks to people who would otherwise suffer the appalling effects of some single gene disease should be minimal.

10.3 If this is so then the damaging situation envisaged in 9.2 would be considerably reduced. In any case the logic of 9.2 might be that much of modern medicine should be abandoned since it allows the weak to survive and even to propagate. There is also the point that what appeared to Ramsey as a 'deteriorating gene pool' might be in reality a more diverse gene pool. As already noted, there is evidence that some single gene 'defects' (e.g. those responsible for sickle cell anaemia) have other effects which are beneficial. Emphasising notions of the common good at the expense of a desire to care for the weak and the disadvantaged would also seem to be an inversion of Christian ethics. Doubtless Christian ethicists do have to consider seriously issues concerned with the common good. Nevertheless they have a primary imperative in Scripture to be concerned for the weak and disadvantaged.

10.4 It is important to keep in mind the distinction made earlier between human germ line treatment (which is still not permitted) and somatic gene therapy (which sometimes is). The latter may soon be able to help those suffering from a variety of inherited disorders caused by a single gene such as cystic fibrosis and some malignant tumours. Although somatic gene therapy is not without risks, it probably raises few new issues for medical ethics – unless the new genes can enter the germ line. In contrast, it is the unknown implications for future generations which create the most acute ethical dilemmas arising from germ line forms of treatment.

10.5 Perhaps even Ramsey's theological arguments are exaggerated. The logic of 9.4 might seem to be that humans should always accept what is there in the biological world as simply God-given. God has ordered sexuality and procreation in this way, so in this way it must remain. Those who reject any form of barrier or hormonal contraception (Ramsey was not amongst them) would seem to accept this proposition more strongly than those who do not. Yet even the former seldom apply this principle to the non-human biological world. Those viruses which are dangerous to human beings, for example, are seldom treated as God-given. Again, much of modern medicine would seem to go against such a principle.

10.6 This last point also suggests a major weakness in 9.5. On the basis of Ramsey's objection it is easy to see that many of the most dramatic developments in medicine over the last quarter-of-a-century might have been disallowed. Heart transplants, which are now almost routine, appeared initially to many as humans attempting to 'play God' before they had learned to be humans. Multi-organ transplants today may still appear in that guise. Yet only by taking such bold steps on patients, who have given informed consent and who would otherwise soon die, can such remarkable surgical achievements be made.

10.7 It might seem, then, that these new fertility and genetic treatments are relatively free of moral and theological difficulties. Provided that society is cautious and ensures that they are fully *and humanely* tested on animals long before they are used on human beings and that, once they are used on human beings, there is a very serious and informed reason for doing so, then it would seem that they are morally permissible.

## Fresh Doubts

11.1 Such a position ignores two other moral doubts that have been raised about such techniques.

11.2 Firstly, there is the question of personal identity. The rapid advances in fertility treatment mean that five different parents have now to be distinguished. Theoretically, at least, a child can have three types of mother (genetic, gestational and social) and two types of father (genetic and social). So, in addition to all of the problems of personal identity encountered by those who have been adopted, these advances in fertility treatment add confusions at both genetic and gestational levels.

11.3 It is possible to exaggerate the novelty of questions of personal identity raised in this area. Genetic paternity was an issue of contention long before the advent of medically supervised AID. Many societies have gone to extraordinary lengths to control the behaviour and freedom of fertile women in order to ensure paternity. Adding genetic and gestational mothers to the list of possible parents clearly extends the problem of personal identity in this area. The difficulty is to know whether such new identity issues are conceptually novel and, as such, discontinuous with those familiar issues arising from adoption and doubts about paternity.

11.4 Secondly, there is the question of precedent. Many fear that advanced forms of fertility treatment and (eventually) genetic surgery having been allowed for exceptional cases will, in turn, become an 'option' for all. Perhaps it is this fear which lay behind many of Paul Ramsey's objections. Compassion for those desperate to have a child (many of whom would make considerably more responsible parents than many teenage single parents) or for families blighted by a single gene defect, acts as the drive to introduce changes in medical practice. Yet, once these changes have been introduced, the resulting techniques might soon become available for all no matter how trivial their reasons might seem.

11.5 An analogy with the Abortion Act of 1967 is again appropriate. Those church leaders who supported a change in legislation at the time usually did so on the basis of hard cases. They seldom argued that abortion was a 'right' for all fertile women. Yet the Act, once introduced, was soon interpreted as allowing for abortion on request at least during the first trimester. In effect it turned a 'liberty' into a 'right'. Undoubtedly this Act has prevented many septic abortions and it is difficult to imagine that it will be repealed. Yet the experience of supporting a change in law on the basis of difficult cases, and then seeing this change extended to many less difficult cases, has made many church leaders wary.

11.6 A further reason for wariness in this area is the potential for political and social abuse. Memories still survive of the eugenic programmes of a number of totalitarian regimes. Real caution is needed in a liberal democracy to ensure that techniques developed for humanitarian reasons do not become instruments of political abuse in other regimes. There is even a danger in a liberal democracy that an understandable popular desire for 'perfect babies' does not become a means of discriminating against those with severe disabilities. The possibility of both political and social eugenics suggests wariness here.

11.7 Should such a wariness extend to the area of advanced forms of fertility and germ line treatment?

11.8 A possible answer is as follows: Yes it should, but the wariness should be addressed more at medical culture than at the law. Perhaps we should distinguish more carefully in this complex area between what is legally permissible and what is medically desirable. Advanced forms of fertility treatment are legally permissible in Britain but they may not always be medically desirable. As means of allowing otherwise infertile couples to have children, they may indeed be justifiable despite their attendant risks to personal identity. Just as those who adopt children know that they must work hard to counter the difficulties of personal identity that their children often feel, so those who have children by means of advanced forms of fertility must act similarly. However, such risks would be distinctly less justifiable if they were to be used by otherwise fertile couples for social or cultural reasons.

11.9 Perhaps this argument can be extended to germ line treatment. Once the physical risks involved in such treatment are understood and minimised from experience in the agricultural world, then it might sometimes be morally justifiable to allow it for those families who would otherwise face grave genetic disabilities. Even though scientists may still be some way from establishing such knowledge (and there must be considerable doubt about the applicability of all agricultural knowledge to humans) or from being able to undertake human genetic surgery, it is possible to foresee an eventual change in regulation and practice in this area. For example, it might become possible safely to eliminate a deficient gene from sperm before implantation (AIH).

11.10 However, even then good medical practice should still ensure that this is an exceptional form of treatment in the absence of safer alternatives to meet a grave and known genetic disability. Three conditions are important here: (*a*) the condition is life-threatening; (*b*) the risks are broadly established (this is likely to be easier for single gene than for polygenetic conditions); (*c*) there is no safer alternative treatment (selective abortion in most cases is likely to be safer – although, of course, it will remain morally unacceptable to some). In short, this is not an option to be made generally available for cultural or social reasons. It is specifically intended as a form of medical treatment designed both to help those families who are gravely at risk and to reduce the possible accumulative genetic deterioration envisaged in 9.2.

11.11 On this narrow basis germ line treatment might one day be judged to be morally justifiable by church leaders.

# 12

# *Religious Education and Postmodernity*

Throughout this book the issue of postmodernity has been a dominant theme. Fragmentation, an incredulity towards meta-narratives, privatisation, eclecticism and, above all, moral relativism and pluralism, have all been identified as features of a postmodern age. Of course, these features can all be exaggerated, by claiming either their ubiquity in the present or their complete absence in the past. Anyone who has read the diaries of Samuel Pepys written in the seventeenth century or those of James Boswell in the eighteenth century will be aware that such 'postmodern' features can certainly be found in the past. And doubtless there are some enclaves of comparative uniformity even within Western society today. In the first chapter it was argued that there is more than one way of understanding postmodernity – for instance, literary and architectural understandings of postmodernity differ from each other. Even the distinction between modernity and post-modernity is itself relative: theologians should beware of hyperbole when depicting present-day culture.[1]

Nevertheless in some areas of culture today *perceptions* of moral relativism and pluralism do seem to be particularly strong. Within religious education it is now a truism that we live in a religiously pluralistic, multi-faith society. Some have argued that this perception may itself be based as much in ideology as in empiricism, since the small presence of non-Christian world faiths in Britain as a whole hardly amounts to

[1] cf. David Tracy, 'Theology and the Many Faces of Postmodernity', *Theology Today*, Vol. 50, No. 1, 1994, pp. 104–14.

'a multi-faith society'.[2] Whether these are perceptions or actualities may not matter here too much, since social perceptions are just as interesting to the sociologist.

In this final chapter I will use the three broad sociological approaches that I first mapped out over twenty years ago[3] and which have structured my research ever since. In the process I will attempt to show how they can be related specifically to the interactions of theology and religious education today.

## 1. The Social Context of Theology

This approach uses mainstream sociology to help theologians to come to a clearer understanding of the broad hermeneutical context within which they must operate. When first mapping out this approach I noted that theologians involved in the 'secular theology' debate of the 1960s made curiously similar assumptions about the nature of society. My interest was particularly in the so-called *Honest to God* debate. What became evident was that the theological protagonists John Robinson[4] and Eric Mascall,[5] although apparently opposed diametrically on theological issues, both assumed that modern theology operated in a radically secularised context. Robinson argued in effect that modern people are fundamentally 'secular', so theology if it is to communicate at all must itself become more secular. It must prune away those mythological features inherited from the first century which no longer seem plausible within the twentieth century. Mascall argued quite oppositely that it was not the business of theologians in any age to 'prune' the faith. Rather they must restate the Gospel in all its fullness. If the twentieth century regarded this as implausible then that was just too bad for the twentieth century. We live in deeply secular times which must be resisted to the full. Indeed, Mascall believed that Robinson and others like him had themselves become a part of the process of secularisation.

---

[2] See Basil Mitchell, *Faith and Criticism*, OUP, Oxford, 1994.
[3] See my *The Social Context of Theology*, Mowbray, Oxford, 1975.
[4] John Robinson, *Honest to God*, SCM Press, London, 1963.
[5] E. L. Mascall, *The Secularisation of Christianity*, Darton, Longman & Todd, London, 1965.

However, reading books in the sociology of religion at the time it soon became obvious that the concept of 'secularisation' was a sociologically contested notion. There were some sociologists such as Bryan Wilson[6] in Britain and Peter Berger[7] in the United States who argued that secularisation was indeed the process that most typified modern society. However, there were others such as David Martin[8] in Britain and, more erratically, Andrew Greeley[9] in the United States who were distinctly sceptical about secularisation as a thoroughgoing, ineluctable process which inevitably followed modernity. Theologians at the time had generally missed the work of this second group of sociologists altogether. Yet over the last two decades – and as a result of some unexpected ambiguities in the data about religion in the 'modern' world – it is this group that has become more dominant within the sociology of religion. Partly as a result of the rise of various forms of religious fundamentalism within apparently 'modern societies', partly as a result of the persistence of less formal types of populist religion (sometimes termed 'folk' religion), and partly as a result of the resurgence of inter-religious warfare in the late twentieth century, critics of the thoroughgoing secularisation model are now in the ascendancy.[10] Even a robust defender of the thoroughgoing secularisation model, such as Steve Bruce, admits that 'not everyone would accept either the general claim that modernization has been accompanied by secularization or all of the elements of the explanation of that process which I have offered'.[11] Whereas a generation ago Wilson could largely ignore sociological critics of the secularisation model, Bruce today has to defend his own position at length against them. That in itself is significant: secularisation is now manifestly a contentious sociological model.

[6] Bryan Wilson, *Religion in Secular Society*, C. A. Watts, London, 1966.
[7] Peter L. Berger, *The Social Reality of Religion*, Faber & Faber, London, 1969.
[8] David Martin, *The Sacred and the Secular*, Routledge & Kegan Paul, London, 1969.
[9] Andrew M. Greeley, *The Persistence of Religion*, SCM Press, London, 1973.
[10] See my *Competing Convictions*, SCM Press, London, 1989.
[11] Steve Bruce, *Religion in the Modern World: From Cathedrals to Cults*, OUP, Oxford, 1996, p. 52.

It is possible that 'secularisation' is no longer a very useful way to depict the social context within which Western theology and religious education must operate today. Quite apart from the ambiguities in the data about religion in the modern world, for many years it has proved remarkably difficult to reach a consensus about what is meant by the term 'secularisation'.[12] Despite its widespread use outside the sociology of religion, it has accrued so many different meanings that it may be more helpful to replace it with other notions which are gaining increasing credibility elsewhere in the social sciences. Chief amongst these is the concept of globalisation. Used alongside notions of post-modernity, globalisation may offer a rather less contentious sociological model to depict the context of religious education today.

Amongst international relations analysts, the concept of globalisation is increasingly being used to analyse interactions between various religions and world-wide social and cultural change.[13] The process of globalisation is particularly evident in international trade, communication and travel. Although there is nothing particularly new about any of these, modern technology does seem to exacerbate their effects. So, whereas the privileged few have long travelled around the world, now international travel is a regular feature for many people within the wealthier nations. And as more and more people travel to hotter (or sometimes cooler) climates for their holidays, so the most expensive and exotic holidays penetrate tribal areas which were once reached only by a handful of missionaries and anthropologists. Even within the last twenty-five years this situation has changed dramatically. In the early 1970s Papua New Guinea was a country that my family visited and worked in for a year with considerable difficulty and much sense of isolation. Recently we returned there for a week and found that exotic tourism had already arrived. Anyone with enough money can now travel to the mangrove swamps of Eastern Papua New Guinea in a style

[12] See Larry Shiner, 'The Meanings of Secularisation', *International Yearbook for the Sociology of Religion*, Vol. III, 1967.

[13] See Roland Robertson, *Globalization: Social Theory and Global Culture*, Sage, London, 1992, and Peter Beyer, *Religion and Globalization*, Sage, London, 1994.

and manner that would have been quite unthinkable less than a generation ago.

It is not too difficult to see that this exacerbated process of travel may have social and cultural effects both upon those who travel and upon those who are visited. Papua New Guinea, like many places in the world, seems to have become more violent in the last quarter of a century and tragically diseases such as AIDS have also been imported there. International hotels, fast food chains, and luxury shops in Port Moresby increasingly resemble their counterparts elsewhere in the world. Even if most people within the local population are too poor to use any of these facilities they are still surrounded by them. A message of acquisitiveness is plain for all to see, both rich and poor, and perhaps as a result the former must live behind ever higher and higher security fences. Life in Port Moresby for professional groups is little different from life in Lusaka. In both places personal security is paramount.

Globalisation is a process that gradually imposes striking uniformities across the globe. The media – especially in the form of satellite television and internationally owned newspapers – are powerful reinforcers of this process. Whether their social and cultural influence is direct or indirect is, of course, an issue of considerable contention amongst social scientists. Without taking sides in this particular debate it is clear that the media are increasingly a feature of globalisation. At the very least they reflect and mirror a shrinking and more uniform world in which local culture and morality become simply matters of personal 'preference'.

This last point has been depicted powerfully in the writings of Peter Berger. In *The Heretical Imperative*[14] he argued that 'modernity' (a term he has used more than globalisation) carries with it a bewildering range of personal 'choices'. If in more traditional societies 'heretics' – that is, from the Greek, the ones who 'chose' – were regarded as deviants, in modern societies heresy becomes the dominant position. We are all forced to make choices at so many different levels and in the process become conscious that personal preference has replaced

[14] Peter L. Berger, *The Heretical Imperative*, Collins, London, 1980.

convention. In his recent *A Far Glory*[15] Berger reflects some of the pain that this brings him in his own relation to religious institutions. In terms of Troeltsch's typology Berger is the lone mystic. Despite being a striking apologist of Christian belief he cannot find a denomination or congregation that pleases him. To this last book he adds a subtitle that indicates his dilemma and with it his shift away from a thoroughgoing secularisation model – *The Quest for Faith in an Age of Credulity*.

Concepts of postmodernity express a rather different set of processes. There is something strikingly affluent about Berger's analysis of modernity. Perhaps he is conscious of enormous choices in his own life, but the experience of many people within post-industrial societies is that they feel that at some levels they have less choice than they might have had in a previous generation. Today they cannot choose to have a secure job, they cannot choose where to live, and many, even within affluent countries, cannot choose to travel wherever they wish. All of these 'choices' require a secure income in a world in which security of income has become increasingly problematic for an increasing number of individuals. At best 'modernity' in this sense expresses only a part of Western experience today – and surely even less of non-Western experience. Personal, rational choice based upon secure affluence is hardly an experience of all, even of the majority, at the end of the twentieth century. Postmodernity suggests rather that fragmentation, non-rationality, resurgent local customs and communities, and the breakdown of post-Enlightenment consensus are also widely present.

As was seen earlier, postmodernity as a concept is used by intellectuals in a bewildering variety of ways.[16] Most post-modernists working from a literary approach agree that any uniform notion of 'truth' or ways of establishing truth (especially those deriving from the Enlightenment) have

[15] Peter L. Berger, *A Far Glory*, Free Press, New York, 1992.

[16] cf. David Harvey, *The Condition of Postmodernity*, Blackwell, Oxford, 1989; Steven Connor, *Postmodernist Culture*, Blackwell, Oxford, 1989; Thomas Docherty (ed), *Postmodernism: A Reader*, Harvester/Wheatsheaf, New York and London, 1993; and Krishan Kumar, *From Post-Industrial to Post-Modern Society: New Theories of the Contemporary World*, Blackwell, Oxford, 1995.

increasingly broken down. Agreed working practices might still be considered to be necessary in practical science, but even these should not be regarded as unchallengable axioms. In most other intellectual areas fragmentation is increasingly evident. However, as seen in the fourth chapter, considerable differences emerge, even for literary postmodernists, on the issues of foundationalism and communitarianism. For some of the most radical postmodernists there are now no common intellectual foundations whatsoever, there are only incommensurable communities of knowledge. For others such features as logic and non-contradiction still survive as bridges between different communities of knowledge, allowing individuals to move between them and even to belong to several different communities simultaneously.

Postmodernists working from a more architectural approach present a rather different picture which has important points of contact with globalisation. Elsewhere[17] I have attempted to define postmodernity from this approach as 'an eclectic borrowing from the past albeit in a modern guise'. Fragmentation or eclecticism is only one feature of this definition. A second feature involves an element of nostalgia. Within architecture postmodernity has been associated with an attempt to revive features from the past – albeit often in a highly eclectic manner. A third feature involves a frank recognition that postmodernity is a process which reacts both against and with modernity. The sheer cost and inconvenience of using older materials consistently in reconstructing features from the past – quite apart from the scarcity of the craft skills that were essential in the past – ensures that modern techniques, materials and con-veniences are still a strong feature of architecture today. Understood in this way postmodernity is a highly complex process with obvious points of contact with modernity or globalisation but also with some sharp differences. Post-modernity tends to emphasise the local rather than the global, the particular rather than the general, the exclusive rather than the inclusive, the distinctive rather than the general.

[17] See my *Moral Communities*, Exeter University Press, Exeter, 1992.

It is precisely these tensions which seem most useful in depicting differing patterns of theology and religious education today. If much of the theological debate in the 1960s assumed that secularisation was an endemic and ubiquitous process, in the 1990s this assumption has become more problematic. It is no longer self-evident that social processes can be adequately depicted in such a monolithic manner. Social processes now seem more ambiguous and sometimes conflictory. Specifically within religious education there seem to be competing demands from, on the one hand, an assertive secular humanism, and, on the other, a recognition of plural religious and ideological traditions.

One way of reducing such tensions and ambiguities on religious issues in the modern world is to *privatise* religious commitments and to study them all equally and dispassionately. Globalisation theory often depicts this as the preferred option in the West. Some postmodern interpretations suggest otherwise, viewing secular humanism itself as a sectarian ideology and seeing conflicts growing between religious and ideological groups with no overall rational resolution of differences between them.

These variant interpretations of social context have radical implications for church leaders and religious education today. For example, the current demand for Islamic schools in Britain and elsewhere, to be financed if possible by the State, fits some forms of postmodernist analysis. Whereas a religious curriculum based upon comparing a series of different religious traditions better fits a globalisation analysis – as does a mode of teaching academic theology which is always conscious of ecumenical variants.

## 2. Social Determinants of Theology

It is now widely recognised that theological positions have social histories. Through the work of New Testament scholars such as Meeks, Gager and Theissen there is now a much broader recognition of the specific communities and social environments that helped to shape some of the diverse features of early Christianity.[18] Social factors are also used to understand better

[18] I analyse these further in *Theology and Sociology*, Chapman, London, 1987 and revised 1996.

the development of doctrine and moral theology over the centuries. If once social 'explanations' were used only in theological polemics, today they are widely used to understand better all theological positions including one's own.

This wider recognition is obviously relevant to present-day church leaders and religious education. Identifying social locations is a part of understanding differing religious traditions and variants within these traditions. And theology as an academic subject, and religious education more widely, can be studied from the perspective of the sociology of knowledge as cognitive disciplines which change diachronically and synchronically. The understanding of academic theology and religious education that each generation has, and even that particular societies have, itself can become the subject of scholarly attention.

However, such scholarly attention also brings with it a number of tensions. The most obvious of these is the tension between freedom and determination. If a discipline is regarded as socially determined, in what sense can 'free enquiry' genuinely take place within it? Another tension is between relativism and objective truth. If everything is regarded as socially relative – including the very academic disciplines themselves – what happens to issues of 'truth' and 'falsity'? Are these to be regarded as relative too? To return again to *Veritatis Splendor*, it captures the dilemma of 'modern' culture:

> Side by side with its exaltation of freedom, yet oddly in contrast with it, modern culture radically questions the very existence of this freedom. A number of disciplines, grouped under the name of the 'behavioural sciences', have rightly drawn attention to the many kinds of psychological and social conditioning which influence the exercise of human freedom . . . But some people, going beyond the conclusions which can be legitimately drawn from these observations, have come to question or even deny the very reality of human freedom.[19]

There is an obvious logical nonsense in adopting a *purely* relativist and determinist position in any discipline (a position that clearly cannot justify itself). Nevertheless, there are many

[19] Pope John-Paul II, *Veritatis Splendor*, Catholic Truth Society, London, 1993.

who adopt a position of methodological (as distinct from ontological) relativism and determinism. That is, they treat religion (and culture generally) as if it is nothing but a product of social factors. Some, working paradoxically in the Enlightenment tradition, regard their own 'dispassionate analysis' as a product of a free enquiry and truth.

Theological maturity within a faith tradition may require both a recognition of the importance of social factors and of the claims of truth.[20] A postmodern perspective, especially one based upon a literary approach, suggests that it is only within a faith tradition that this balance might be fully achieved. Religion is not something that can be assessed adequately on a dispassionate basis. As was seen earlier, for the most radical postmodernists, there is no purely 'neutral' way of understanding and assessing religious issues. A corollary of this is that religious education would be misconceived if it was thought to be a 'neutral' discipline. From such a postmodern perspective a wholly dispassionate approach to religious education would be doomed to failure.

### 3. Social Significance of Theology

Whilst a thoroughgoing secularisation model reigned amongst intellectuals there was no reason for them to regard religious issues as significant in the modern world. At best academic theology, and more widely religious education, could be seen as ways of better understanding a world that is now past. They might still inform private conscience, but they are no longer socially significant.

On this understanding the dramatic rise of Iranian fundamentalism, for example, was typically regarded as a passing epiphenomenon. Indeed, before 1979 few political analysts (trained as they usually were in a secular mode) predicted the overthrow of the Shah and the subsequent reversal of secular liberalism in Iran.[21] Similarly Muslim offence throughout Europe at Salman Rushdie's *The Satanic Verses* has often

---

[20] cf. Kieran Flanagan, *The Enchantment of Sociology: A Study of Theology and Culture*, Macmillan Press, 1996.
[21] See further my *Competing Convictions*.

been depicted as a 'medieval aberration'. Typically within this perspective literary freedom is regarded as paramount, whilst offended religious sensitivities are manifestly not. Curiously secularists often regard race and gender as areas of legitimate offence, but seldom regard blasphemy as anything other than local idiosyncrasy.

Again a postmodern, literary-based perspective typically views these issues rather differently. The implicit values of a dominant secular humanism (autonomy, personal freedom, tolerance, and so forth) – which have done so much to shape modern Europe – can no longer be assumed. The more jagged edges of conflictual religious traditions are once again taken more seriously. Understanding religion within both academic theology and religious education both becomes more important within the academy and becomes a matter of taking sharp differences more seriously.[22]

Here too, a number of tensions may be identified. There is the tension between ecumenism and increasingly funda-mentalisms. There is also a tension between theological order/consensus and conflict. And there is a tension between what is often identified sociologically as 'inclusivism' and 'exclusivism'.

If ecumenism seemed to be the dominant path of religious traditions in the 1960s (which some linked to secularisation and others to globalisation),[23] the 1980s and 1990s have seen a sharp resurgence of more conservative religious traditions in many parts of the world. Within Christianity in many parts of Europe, and indeed within both Christianity and Islam in many parts of the world, it is conservative congregations which tend to grow. With this growth is often associated an apparent rise in conflict and exclusivism. Ironically, a postmodern age often looks to religious leaders for enduring values and for a moral order that individualistic secularism is seen to have eroded. Yet the very traditions that these leaders

[22] cf. Edward Farley, *The Fragility of Knowledge: Theological Education in the Church and the University*, Fortress Press, Philadelphia, 1988, and Rebecca Chopp, 'Emerging Issues and Theological Education', *Theological Education*, Spring 1990, pp. 106–24.
[23] See Bryan S. Turner, 'The sociological Explanation of Ecumenicalism', in C. L. Mitton (ed), *The Social Sciences and the Churches*, T&T Clark, Edinburgh, 1972.

represent, in turn, sometimes respond in conflictual and exclusivist ways.

In this situation religious education soon becomes an object of political attention. So in Britain today politicians often wish religious education in schools to be re-enforced precisely in order to engender moral order into what appears to be an increasingly anomic society. Yet religious educationalists themselves frequently reject such a functionalist understanding of their discipline. Those schooled in the ways of dispassionate analysis tend to regard it as an ideological intrusion. Whereas those working explicitly within a faith tradition may regard it as a misunderstanding of the nature of faith, since it gives priority to moral rather than to theological factors. However, both groups surprisingly find themselves as exponents of a discipline that is now regarded as politically important . . . that is to say, as socially significant. And that surely is new!

# Conclusion

There are many similarities between this book and my earlier collection *Christian Ethics in Secular Worlds* as well as some important differences. Both books emphasise the crucial role of communities, and especially worshipping communities, in Christian ethics. Both show my debt to Alasdair MacIntyre and to the debate that he has generated. And both express my conviction that the Christian ethicist should attempt to engage distinctively with secular thought in a variety of areas and as inclusively as possible. However, there are also some differences. In the present book I take more seriously notions of postmodernity and the specific dilemmas that it poses for church leadership. It is this last element that helps to integrate research that until recently I have been doing in rather separate areas.

Initially there was a single strand to my research. In my earliest books *The Social Context of Theology* (1975), *Theology and Social Structure* (1977) and *Prophecy and Praxis* (1981) I was concerned to explore how theologians might make better use of sociology within their discipline. Rather than regarding sociology as an alien discipline, I sought to show how a judicious use of its insights might help the theological task. The first edition of my reader *Theology and Sociology* (1987) attempted to provide an overview of different ways of achieving this. At the time this alliance appeared relatively secure. However, a new edition of this reader (1996) suggests that this appearance of security was mistaken: it now includes a more disruptive section on postmodernity within the two disciplines.

The tensions of postmodernity are also reflected in my *Readings in Modern Theology* (1995).

By the mid-1980s my research was beginning to divide into two. One strand, although still making considerable use of sociology, was primarily concerned with Christian ethics. First I produced the polemical *The Cross Against the Bomb* (1984) and then the more sedate *A Textbook of Christian Ethics* (1985 and revised 1995). After that came *Christian Ethics in Secular Worlds* (1991) and *Moral Communities* (1992). The other strand, however, was concerned with church structures. A polemical work again started this particular strand, in this instance *Beyond Decline* (1988). This book led directly to the research into churchgoing patterns and church structures that I did in my four years at Newcastle University and was published first in *Competing Convictions* (1989) and then at considerable length in *The Myth of the Empty Church* (1993). A short, derivative book written for congregations, *A Vision for Growth* (1994), sought to bring this strand of research to a conclusion.

But there was still a gap. I had done little research on leadership in relation to changing church structures. Working on this theme I at last realised that the two strands needed to come back together, since church leaders manifestly should be concerned about both structural and moral leadership. The result of this belated realisation is the short book that I wrote with Derek Burke, *Strategic Church Leadership* (1996) as well as this present book on moral leadership. Together they represent these two vital aspects of church leadership.

Now at last I can see more clearly how I should write *Moral Communities and Christian Ethics*. I think that it ought to have both empirical and meta-ethical components. Originally I had conceived of it being concerned only with the latter, in line with the other contributions to the Cambridge University Press series *New Studies in Christian Ethics*. Yet the obvious gap in the literature is a serious study of moral communities not just as they *should* be but also as they actually *are*. More specifically, is there any empirical evidence that the key theological features of faith, hope and love are in reality characteristic of churches as moral communities? And if there is any data to be found in this area, how does it relate to the post-MacIntyre debate within

Christian ethics? I am only too conscious of the considerable amount of work needed if these questions are to be answered adequately. They should certainly keep me occupied. These are exciting times for Christian ethics.

# INDEX

# Index